Out of the Depths

The *Daily Telegraph* Meditations

Edward Norman

CONTINUUM
London and New York

Continuum
The Tower Building, 11 York Road, London SE1 7NX
370 Lexington Avenue, New York NY 10017-6503

British Library Cataloguing-in-Publication Data
A catalogue record for this book is available from the British Library.

0-8264-5399-6

Typeset by BookEns Ltd, Royston, Herts
Printed and bound in Great Britain by
TJ International Ltd., Padstow, Cornwall

Contents

Introduction   ix

1. The message not the medium – 3 October 1992   1
2. The need to learn – 10 October 1992   3
3. Wrong priorities – 17 October 1992   5
4. The divine gift – 31 October 1992   7
5. Private enterprise religion – 14 November 1992   9
6. Another world to stand upon – 28 November 1992   11
7. The return of the dove to the ark – 5 December 1992   13
8. Peace on earth – 19 December 1992   15
9. The year of the Lord – 2 January 1993   17
10. Easter Eve – 10 April 1993   19
11. As we forgive them that trespass – 24 April 1993   21
12. Community care – 1 May 1993   23
13. Community truth – 8 May 1993   25
14. Community illusions – 15 May 1993   27
15. The hope of sinners – 22 May 1993   29
16. To seek and to save that which was lost –
    5 June 1993   31
17. Putting up with imperfection – 19 June 1993   33
18. Take nothing for your journey – 3 July 1993   35
19. The human God – 9 October 1993   37
20. Window into heaven – 23 October 1993   39
21. The poverty of understanding – 30 October 1993   41
22. Weeping over the city of Jerusalem –
    6 November 1993   43
23. The vocabulary of prayer – 13 November 1993   45
24. The moral norms – 4 December 1993   47

v

25. The pearl of little price – 25 December 1993   49
26. National crime – 23 April 1994   51
27. Out of the depths – 30 April 1994   53
28. The kingdom of God – 7 May 1994   55
29. They know not what they do – 21 May 1994   57
30. The Trinity of love – 28 May 1994   59
31. Marching as to war – 11 June 1994   61
32. The value of time – 18 June 1994   63
33. Faith which is truth – 25 June 1994   65
34. Faith which is demanding – 2 July 1994   67
35. The wonderful and great mystery – 8 October 1994   69
36. Dust before the wind – 22 October 1994   71
37. For all the saints – 29 October 1994   73
38. The sheepfold of truth – 3 December 1994   75
39. Called to our lower natures – 17 December 1994   77
40. The end of the year – 31 December 1994   79
41. False priorities – 8 April 1995   81
42. Easter renewal – 15 April 1995   83
43. Where is thy sting? – 22 April 1995   85
44. The spiritual adventurers – 6 May 1995   87
45. The darkening horizon – 13 May 1995   89
46. Triumph of the Ascension – 27 May 1995   91
47. The gift of the Spirit – 3 June 1995   93
48. In sickness and in health – 10 June 1995   95
49. Proclaiming the truth – 24 June 1995   97
50. Being born again – 12 June 1995   99
51. A lost generation – 21 October 1995   101
52. The unreal world – 4 November 1995   103
53. Understanding the world – 11 November 1995   105
54. Whoever is perfect among you – 18 November 1995   107
55. The earthly snare – 16 December 1995   109
56. Something to be thankful for – 13 April 1996   111
57. On leaving the world – 20 April 1996   113
58. Enduring truths – 27 April 1996   115
59. Relative judgements – 11 May 1996   117
60. Called by love – 18 May 1996   119
61. Master and friend – 22 June 1996   121
62. Divine essentials – 29 June 1996   123
63. The last are first – 6 July 1996   125
64. The world as it is – 12 October 1996   127

vi

65. There abide until you depart – 19 October 1996   129
66. Living love – 26 October 1996   131
67. All Souls – 2 November 1996   133
68. Intercession – 16 November 1996   135
69. The rule of life – 23 November 1996   137
70. Now and ever shall be – 14 December 1996   139
71. The star of Bethlehem – 21 December 1996   141
72. Forgiving past wrongs – 28 December 1996   143
73. Liberation from sin – 4 January 1997   145
74. Sin – 26 April 1997   147
75. Ascended and glorified – 10 May 1997   149
76. Whitsun Eve – 17 May 1997   151
77. A glimpse into the inferno – 31 May 1997   153
78. Service – 7 June 1997   155
79. The self-remedy that fails – 14 June 1997   157
80. Love of strangers – 21 June 1997   159
81. The enemy within – 28 June 1997   161
82. The emptiness within – 11 October 1997   163
83. Healing with a purpose – 18 October 1997   165
84. All Saints – 1 November 1997   167
85. Death wish – 8 November 1997   169
86. An intimidating new world – 22 November 1997   171
87. Changing times – 29 November 1997   173
88. At the year's end – 27 December 1997   175
89. The end of life – 3 January 1998   177
90. The Resurrection of Christ – 11 April 1998   179
91. The burden that is light – 18 April 1998   181
92. A discipline for the soul – 25 April 1998   183
93. A morality for all seasons – 16 May 1998   185
94. The teaching of Christ – 23 May 1998   187
95. The vocation of interpretation – 13 June 1998   189
96. Wheat and tares – 20 June 1998   191
97. Forgiveness – 24 October 1998   193
98. Keeping the truth – 7 November 1998   195
99. Declaring Christ – 14 November 1998   197
100. Thy will be done – 12 December 1998   199
101. The eternal hope – 2 January 1999   201
102. The true cost of virtue – 17 April 1999   203
103. Taking up the Cross – 24 April 1999   205
104. Dust to dust – 8 May 1999   207

105. Raised to glory – 15 May 1999   209
106. How to know God – 26 June 1999   211
107. The mercy of God – 3 July 1999   213
108. Not having everything – 9 October 1999   215
109. More than human need – 16 October 1999   217
110. A diminished state – 6 November 1999   219
111. Remembrance – 13 November 1999   221
112. Family values – 20 November 1999   223
113. Accepting ourselves – 27 November 1999   225
114. The mote and the beam – 4 December 1999   227
115. A clear message – 18 December 1999   229
116. Christmas cheer – c. 25 December 1999   231
117. Millennium blues – 1 January 2000   233
118. Human disobedience – 8 April 2000   235
119. The kingdom of heaven is at hand – 15 April 2000   237
120. Triumph over death – 22 April 2000   239
121. Universal sin – 29 April 2000   241
122. Living with sin – 6 May 2000   243
123. Ruler of the heart – 13 May 2000   245
124. More than a token – 20 May 2000   247
125. Moral confusion – 27 May 2000   249
126. Raised to glory – 3 June 2000   251
127. Wrong perspectives – 10 June 2000   253
128. The mirror of imperfection – 17 June 2000   255
129. Clear advice – 24 June 2000   257
130. Sacrifice – 1 July 2000   259

Introduction

ဆာරය

Looking back over these pieces of writing from the perspective of the past ten years, it is impossible not to be impressed by how greatly, even in such a relatively short space of time, the religious context has changed. The confidence of the British Churches in their own message, never in modern times particularly secure, has drained away still further; the people to whom they seek to address themselves appear even less liable than once they were to turn to institutional religion as the vehicle of their moral seriousness or their spiritual instincts. The 1990s was proclaimed as the 'Decade of Evangelism'; it proved, in the event, to witness an accelerating sequence of decline.

In the longest view, it may well prove to have been a decisive moment in the replacement of Christianity by a version of materialist humanism as the staple reference in the conduct of public affairs. There have, of course, been numerous long-term indications that something of the sort was occurring – extending back more than a century. And the common use of the rhetorical styles and the verbal imagery of the Christian religion have been, and are still likely to be for a time, widely canvassed to articulate sacral values. The basic process, however, has been a secularization of the culture, and an astonishing internal dismantling of the faith by many of its own leaders. Humanism could always be assailed when it was the preserve of intellectuals; throughout much of the last century it was usefully incorporated into the moral system of the Marxists, and while the Cold War existed a non-religious view of humanity, with an accompanying non-religious frame of moral reference, could thus be easily identified. In the last ten years or so, on the other hand, Marxism has blown away as an immediate threat to religious belief but left in its place an understanding of human life which is, in its way, even more threatening to authentic spirituality. For the materialist humanism which now seems to be in ascendancy throughout Western societies has no philosophical label by which it can be identified; it has no recognized system of ideas as its basis: it thrives on the practical appeal of welfare and rights, of enthusiasm for humanity, and an elevated estimate of the capability of society to order itself without resort to transcendent verities. It represents, in fact, the deification of humanity, and it may be recognized in the elevation of welfare above ideology. There are, of course, many self-deceptions in this: a clear set of ideological presuppositions fuels the new humanism, but the extent of the prevalent ideological incoherence makes the present mode seem to be practical or pragmatic rather than theoretical in inspiration. Hence the impatience with religious difference – the welfare of men and women, it is contended, is far more important than mere differences over religious opinion and practice. Religion, indeed, is now being reassessed as the cause of past conflict, the harbinger of superstition, the enemy of intellectual enlightenment. Such sentiments reflect, also, the privatizing of faith which has occurred. Religion is increasingly regarded as a matter for individual selection and judgement, and the relativizing effect of the present moment of intellectual culture prompts the widespread disposition to suppose all religions are of more or less equal value. At the same time the teaching of Christianity in the schools has been replaced by a broad introduction to all the major religious bodies. The practical result is that Hinduism, Islam, Buddhism and Judaism are represented with careful respect – and in a manner safely sanitized to omit any suggestion of illiberal ideas – in order to avoid giving offence to the ethnic minorities who are the principal practitioners. That is very laudable. But Christianity is simultaneously represented amidst a mass of criticisms of its past social record, its supposed cultural insensitivity, its imagined espousal of past errors. The result upon children is doubtless merely intellectual confusion; it does mean, however, that society is not passing on Christianity to the future generations. Nor, evidently, are the Churches.

Very little provision is made by the Church of England to teach its own members the nature of Christian truth. In institutional terms the world of higher learning still has chaplaincies, but departments of theology in the universities have been secularized. Unlike the Catholic Church in many countries, the Church of England has not established an institution to provide a scholarly resource for itself, and still relies on what is left of its presence in the secular universities. Its own network of church schools have long since separated sacred and secular teaching; they no longer make serious arrangements to guarantee that the teachers appointed in them are believers, and have been, largely for funding reasons, assimilated to the prevailing secularization of the state system. Many will dissent from that conclusion; yet the ignorance of what Christianity is all about which characterizes the children who are educated in the church schools is itself sufficient testimony to their general ineffectiveness as transmitters of the faith to the future. It is also disagreeable to have to conclude that probably a large majority of those who actually worship in the pews week by week are fearfully unacquainted with the fundamental doctrines. Nor are they likely to get them from the kind of sermons they hear – which seem heavily dependent on the same welfare priorities as describe the prevalent secular moralism. The truth is that modern people are coming to redefine Christianity as an affair of moral elevation, aesthetic sensation, and emotional sustenance. They seem to select elements according to private disposition and to claim the resulting collection as 'Christianity'. The English people have never been especially marked for their grasp of religious ideas; those of the present era do not even know what they are supposed to be looking for.

The leaders of the Church themselves tend to associate basic Christianity with the most transient varieties of secular moral enthusiasm. The welfare priorities of the present political culture are identified by them – plainly without copious reflection – as practical applications of the love of neighbour enjoined by Christ. They, too, show impatience with those whose insistence on doctrine seems archaic, an unnecessary spiritual obscurantism in a world of pressing social need. It does not occur to them that the benign face of modern humanism disguises rank materialism, a philosophical view of humanity which prioritizes the welfare needs of men and women above their need for repentance and forgiveness. The words 'moral' and 'spiritual' are often employed interchangeably by them, indeed, and the whole concept of spirituality has been secularized. Observers of national education often cite the provision made for 'spiritual' cultivation as evidence of persisting provision for religion – unaware, presumably, that by 'spiritual' those who frame the curricula actually mean whatever elevates the human spirit. By this they intend art and music and personal development, not religion in any recognizably traditional acceptance.

Many of these features have been around for a long time, and some have important and virtuous consequences. Welfare is always a benefit. What is at issue is the descent into a form of materialism which is without articulated philosophical pedigree, and so cannot be readily scrutinized, and a common assumption that practical welfare is morally self-explanatory. The Churches, by failing to witness, as once they did, to the sheer sinfulness of men and women are failing, also, in their sacred vocation. The first call of Jesus was to repentance, not to increased housing benefit or a reduction in hospital waiting lists. These other things are desirable in themselves, and they certainly do not want for advocates. The Church of Christ, however, is the actual presence in the world of a Saviour whose truths are primarily addressed not to the material dislocations of the passing ages, nor to the claims of men and women for security and repose, but to their flawed spiritual condition. The writings which follow attempt to clarify ways in which the great love of God is directed at creatures whose priorities are forever disordered and whose instinct for materialism, in the authentic philosophical sense, is always obtruding, taking different forms in each moment and location. Christians are called to be those who can discern everlasting truths in the transience of things, to see prophetically the beginning of a universal coherence in the chaotic fragments of present understanding. They also know that humanity, both because of its nature and because of its record, deserves nothing. The great mission prayer of St Francis Xavier reminds us that we are to love God without thought of reward. It reminds us, additionally, that before we loved God, he loved us.

Secularization is a subtle process, difficult to analyse, teasing the minds of some of the greatest social scientists by its complexity. In our day the rapid passage into an enhanced secularity is no clearer for all its enlarged scale. The secularization of life proceeds with no boundary-marker, Christian believers themselves sharing so many of the prevailing enthusiasms for humanity which describe its essence. A real ideological battle proceeds almost unnoticed. People nevertheless regret the passing of Christian faith as a distinctive feature of social association in Western societies. They do not typically support a particular Church, and most have never worshipped regularly. Their sorrow at the slipping away from public consciousness of the last remnants of a Christian spiritual presence is real enough, however. Secularization is a matter of lost habit with us, not a conscious reorientation of life and thought. And the Church of Christ will also itself endure, for it is the perpetuation of the work performed for humanity at the Incarnation itself. It is as well to remember that the numbers who constituted the Church were once able to meet in an upper room, so small were they. Whatever the future holds, the purposes of God will certainly prevail. The writings which follow were addressed to Christian believers to help them in their faith, and to any who may by chance read those words in the hope of finding some reflections of Christian understanding, some way of discovering what Christians believe. If the general world-picture presented here supposes, as it does, a perpetual conflict of ideologies, my purpose in writing has been to try to assist those who want to know how the faith may be interpreted as a shield to error. The images of conflict are used frequently in the Bible, and they stand in some contrast to the emollient phrases in appraisal of human claims and human capabilities which are the commonplace moral declamations of our own times.

The *Daily Telegraph* is the last of the English newspapers to carry, each week, a short essay intended to help people in their understanding of Christianity. These Meditations are contributed independently by two ministers, each of whom furnishes texts for half of the year. The present collection of mine is drawn from the last nine years, a selection which necessarily involves some repetitions of themes but which seeks to place more permanently before the reader some of the major dimensions of the faith which this age particularly needs, in my view, to have restated. It is as well always to remember that amidst the spiritual *anomie* of the present time, and despite the seemingly impenetrable solidity of modern materialism, the religion of Jesus endures in all its integrity. It has in every time encountered threats of equal seriousness. It is just that those who seek to be faithful followers of Jesus often lack the self-confidence to recognize the everlasting supremacy of the Faith. And that is because it is, quite simply, true. The following brief essays are offered in order to assist the identification of erroneous ideas about God, so that the authentic serenity of his presence in the world of our experience may be more effectually present to our understanding. Then the world's agenda can be set aside: 'not my will, but yours, be done'.

EDWARD NORMAN
York Minster
July 2000

One

The message not the medium

ಐⱭಚ

There is a rather wistful assumption made by Christians today about the cause of surrounding unbelief that requires to be questioned. It is that the public *image* of religion is to blame: that if only the product could be packaged in a manner more appropriate to popular culture, or to the prevailing intellectual culture, then it would find widespread acceptance. This notion is derived from an imperfect understanding of the nature of Christianity itself. For the hard truth is that Jesus did not come into this world of human insensitivities and appalling brutalities in order to prop up our sense of self-worth and self-entitlement, but to convict us of our sins and to offer the free gift of forgiveness. There is something terrifyingly wrong in the very centre of human life: the frailties and corruptions of all of us are not the consequence of chance personal circumstance or wrong choices but define the way we actually are. Now the last thing people in contemporary Western society want to be told is that they are a texture of interior and structural error, standing in need of external correction by a sovereign who is outside their manipulation.

Modern men and women see themselves as morally autonomous creatures; their dignity and worth, they believe, require attention, not denial – they see life as a catalogue of personal entitlements. The message of their inherent sinfulness is not what they want to hear, and the more explicitly the Church represents its unique insight into the way things are, the less, not the more, people are likely to be attracted. The duty of the Church is not to accommodate the prevailing sense of human self-importance, but to criticize it. To receive authentic Christianity people need to be convinced of their own sin. That was never more difficult than at the present time, when the contemporary culture, both popular and intellectual, is proclaiming to people that their demands for personal fulfilment are in some sense legitimate because of their essential worth as humans.

It has often been said that an age is defined by its doctrine of humanity: ours consecrates the sovereignty of mankind. Our higher rhetoric is all about human rights. But God calls us as his creatures, to recognize our need not for autonomy but for dependence on him. The very clarity of the message is the problem; people today do not want to be dependent – not even on God. And we are his children. Of such is the kingdom of heaven. The message of Jesus is as it has always been: to receive his gift of forgiveness with the simplicity of children.

Two

The need to learn

❧☙

When one of the components of a received culture gets knocked out, or removes itself from the scene, the result is not a vacuum. The other components close up and fill the gap. It is so with religion. Modern Christians are rather given to asserting that there is a kind of natural 'religious' faculty in men and women, and their fear is not that religion will disappear but that its substitutes will be at best inappropriate and at worst positively sinister. Now there are indeed many contemporary substitutes for religion, but they are not filling a gap allocated in the structural composition of human nature: they are, on the contrary, artefacts of human culture, creations in honour of the human claim that human life has dignity and purpose. In that sense the modern substitutes for religion are a parody of religion – and a materialist one too. They express an inclination to suppose that religion was in effect invented by our earliest ancestors as a way of centralizing humanity in what otherwise must seem a hostile and meaningless arrangement of things.

In traditional theology God was certainly known about through his presence in the creation that was the work of his hands – he was known 'naturally'. This was a latent knowledge, however; it described aspects of life in the world. Christians believe that, but they also believe that the active part of religion comes from revelation; that God intervened in his own material creation to reveal aspects of his nature and his gifts to mankind that could only be known about through this special dispensation. To simplify: the Old Testament unfolds the mechanics of God's revelation of himself, and the New Testament discloses the fulness of God's gifts. The Old is about the relationship between God and man, and the New is about salvation. Revealed truth is by its very nature special and exclusive. The early Church, in fact, like the other religious cults of its time, laid great emphasis on the need for initiation into its truths, and for a long and sustained process whereby those truths were learned. And that is precisely what is absent today. Modern people assume that judgements about the truth of Christianity can be made without specialist data. They believe that although materialist culture has filled up the gap left by the collapse of traditional religion they can nevertheless assess religion fairly with the alien intellectual instruments it provides. Modern Christians are themselves astonishingly ill-informed about their own religion. What the Churches and society now need is a great programme of religious education – conducted by the Churches themselves. We are what we take in. The spiritual sustenance we presently receive is not enough to sustain either spiritual vitality or religious understanding.

Three

Wrong priorities

෨෮

The soul of the deceased Marxist empire has not passed from
the world: it has migrated to the West, where it now inhabits
the bodies of the liberal democracies. Economic determinism
and historical materialism are alive and well and flourishing
here. They are expressed in the political priorities of both
governments and governed; they are implicit in the intellectual
culture disseminated in the schools. People judge political
leadership according to its capacity to deliver economic policy,
and their sense of the moral worth of political society is
rendered within a tariff of welfare benefits. There is no clear
ideological purpose to which human society is seen to be
drawn. Neither public figures nor individuals appear to expect
society collectively to promote ultimate goals for life on earth.
For most, it seems, the end of life is the pursuit of happiness,
and the purpose of government is the provision of material
benefits. With what sardonic humour the Marxist thinkers of
the past must look down upon the fate of Western society! The
totalitarianism of political ideology has been, at least for a time,
defeated; but in its place there reigns the anonymous
sovereignty of a less well-defined but not less pervasive
materialism. And, as always in human affairs, the victims are
willing agents in their own submission. When the Communist
empire collapsed in eastern Europe less than two years ago
there was a thin cladding, in each country, of philosophical
moralizing. What really happened, however, was a rush to
abandon philosophical materialism for actual materialism: the
demand was not that human society should diminish its

enthusiasm for economic priorities but that the ones adopted should be more successful.

It is, sadly, exactly the same with individual human lives. Men and women are forever ignoring their higher natures in order to satisfy their lower. They so readily become preoccupied with the material requirements of the moment. The process is usually undramatic and comes disguised, even for the most self-conscious, by a propensity to suppose that the cultivation of aesthetic appreciation, or a concern for human welfare, are themselves higher goals. But they are not, at least in themselves. They can be, and very commonly are, just another way of defining human life in material values – and neither has much effect, whatever their enthusiasts claim, in elevating the human personality.

The Saviour spoke about the seed that withered because it fell on stony ground, and about the seed which was choked because it fell among thorns. In the parable of the sower, in fact, the seed is the Word of God and we are the ground. Ground needs to be prepared. In our Western societies today, as in our own lives, we make demands about the seed yet neglect the preparation of the ground. So much for the use we make of the freedoms which are the great achievement of liberal and democratic society.

Four

The divine gift

ℰℭ

The great love of God is this: that the eternal and supreme mover of the universe involves himself with each of us. Across the vast spaces he comes to say, in the words of Jesus, that 'even the very hairs of your head are all numbered'. And of course we are not worth it. Neither the human record nor the melancholy facts of individual lives warrant a personal relationship with the infinite presence – but that is precisely what God calls us to receive. It is not the gift of reason, nor the capacity to utilize the materials of the world in the furtherance of human society, nor even the aesthetic and reflective faculties, which allow men and women to know God. It is because God comes to them as a person, and a person who holds out a relationship.

That is how the citizens of the world, for all their spiritual frailty, are able to achieve the serene dignity of becoming the citizens of eternity; how they are able, also, to recognize that the barrier between present experience and the astonishing splendour of the celestial order is penetrable. God became man. In Christ the very vocabulary that the people of the world had used to describe the evidences of the divine was confirmed, and the symbols and images through which the otherwise unknowable categories of heaven could be expressed in earthly terms were given a sure foundation. The universal had become particular, the seen and the unseen worlds were joined, the wistful aspirations of the creatures of the dust were converted into a dialogue with ultimate truth.

The divine essence is all-sufficient. God does not need us.

His truth and his nature do not depend upon our claims to personal significance or claims to interior cultivation or to explanations of reality. We are beckoned towards a destiny that is not of our making. Yet we are forever treating religious truth as if it was especially fashioned to be a prop to our needs; it is as if we expect religion to be a sort of quality addictive, guaranteeing emotional satisfaction. The Christianity of the modern world is becoming a dimension of therapy. Even the clergy tend to define religion as human welfare, and to regard the emotional requirements of the believers as sovereign. But the relationship God holds out is one achieved through our obedience, through our denial of our personal claims to emotional or other satisfaction. The vision of eternity is not the enrichment of our personalities but the stark realization of our worthlessness; the celestial and divine society is glimpsed in time by those whose timelessness derives from the emptying out of human priorities.

Five

Private enterprise religion

ಬಿಣಚಿ

There is a secondary world of personal fulfilment which they inhabit who are disappointed by their experience of the real one: the lonely who would be loved by someone; the ugly who desire beauty; the ambitious whose aspirations are never accomplished; the very many who had expected life to provide continuing enrichment but for whom the earth itself no longer seems a home. These are the citizens of a vanished paradise, a country of the imagination. For them, also, there is a risk that religious belief may become a compensation for the cruelties of failed expectations, an image to succeed the broken hopes.

There is, that is to say, a strong tendency in modern society for individuals to fashion religion for themselves. It becomes a dimension of the pursuit of personal fulfilment. Religious discipline, as a concept, has largely disappeared: religious belief is no longer envisaged as a series of duties and obligations owed to the divine sovereign. It is regarded, on the contrary, as an adjunct to the development of the personality – it is only to be taken up if it does something to satisfy individual requirements for a full and satisfying life. In modern society emotions themselves are indulged as a matter of entertainment; people often expect the same kind of aesthetic or pleasurable sensations from religion that they derive from the performing arts or from warm human relationships. Religion is thus made to serve purely personal ends. We make a god to fit our needs, and his laws are whatever satisfies our demand for meaning or significance. So Christianity becomes a matter of emotional preference, and people shop around to find a version of the faith, or a particular church, which seems to offer fulfilment.

This situation stems ultimately from the decay of traditional society – where religious belief and observance was collective. Regional groups and political units adopted religion as an expression of their collective identity. There was much that was wrong about that; but the modern substitute is no improvement. Now religion has been individualized, and each person feels free to tailor a version of religious faith suited to his personal expectations of life. As those expectations are themselves usually untutored by any acquaintance with spiritual knowledge the result is a random assemblage of ephemeral values. But Christianity is objectively true. It is not the servant of our emotional needs. It proclaims laws made known to us by God, and calls us to the discipline and self-denial of obeying injunctions which our wills often do not find personally conducive, or our emotions instantly satisfying.

Six

Another world to stand upon

 හටක්‍ෂ

For many Christians today their understanding of the faith is most fully expressed through involvement with the problems of society. Theirs is a religion of issues. The teachings of Jesus are seen to have immediate application in matters of justice, and the Church is represented as an agency for human welfare. The spiritualized Christ of past tradition, who beckoned men and women to another world, is abandoned, and the Christ of compassion, who came to bind up the wounds of the afflicted, is identified among the crowds in the market place. There is much to commend this emphasis: it gives real content to spirituality, and helps believers to serve Christ through the service of their brothers and sisters. A Christian life which is not in some sense dedicated to the love of neighbour is not authentic.

But there is an aspect of the Saviour's message which is now too often neglected. He spoke also of the need to live life as an anticipation of eternity. The very concept of 'eternal life' indicates a quality or property of life in the world – it is to be an existence redolent of the spaciousness of eternity. The kingdom of heaven is a present reality. It is experienced, certainly, in one dimension, in the love of neighbour; but it is also experienced, and essentially, in a dimension of detachment from the world. Jesus himself lived independently of many of the conventions of his age; he had no wife, no home, no religious institution which conveyed his supreme truths. About his life there hung no atmosphere of integration with the values of society – whose impending demise, indeed, he predicted. 'Foxes have holes, the birds of the air have nests,' he declared, 'but the Son of man has nowhere to lay his head.'

Detachment from the world is not much valued in contemporary Christianity. The priority is activism, engagement with the world. Yet that very involvement so easily converts into actual worldliness, as participation in the world's agenda of justice and welfare gradually comes to preoccupy our lives. Then the dimension of eternity is lost from sight. The troubles of human society are permanent. The expectations of people are unstable, and what seems acceptable to one age may seem intolerable to another; the claims which are made by some are forever contested by others. All the buzzing enthusiasm for social activism does nothing about the basic desolation of human lives – the interior disjointedness, and the dreadful ambiguity of our natures, to which the insights of religious truth are primarily directed. The message of salvation involves a measure of detachment from the world – St Philip Neri called it *staccamento*. It is the pearl of great price.

Seven

The return of the dove
to the ark

ৠৎ

Modern people seem to have a great capacity for representing commonplace human instincts as virtues. They are, for example, constantly elevating ordinary acts of kindness, and concern for the welfare of others, to the status of heroic morality. Evidences of decent behaviour, which in the ancient world was regarded as simply a definition of being a human rather than a beast, are among us trumpeted as achievements of social compassion and concern. It is as if in the world without God's sovereignty the instinct of charity has been touched by a secular chrism; the great organizations which now exist to stir the public conscience over particular social ills or personal disabilities have succeeded the Church as the place where public virtue finds its higher note. In the religion of humanity the charities are temples of human goodness. Their censorious rejection of those who disagree with their diagnoses of public policy is equal to any dogmatic certainties once given off by the Christian clergy. They enjoy enormous prestige, and do much good. To acquire moral iridescence governments must be respectfully attentive to their propaganda, for the charities are the nearest that modern society gets to a perception of holiness.

What is distinctive about them, however, is that the contemporary elevation of human decency does not involve personal transformation. The outpourings of the moralists are taken at face value: no one asks questions about the moral

13

references in the lives of the moral practitioners – that would be regarded, by us, as disagreeably illiberal – and no one bothers to call upon them to give a name or a pedigree to the moral tradition to which their much publicized concern for humanity belongs. We see, apparently, no necessary relationship between individual worth and moral truth. Anyone who declares himself for humanity gets our approval.

The Christian religion, in contrast, is addressed to those who are quite unable to be consistently moral or decent. It recognizes human moral frailty and asks of its would-be adherents not the enunciation of a morally correct programme but simple repentance. Essays in moral goodness should follow, yet human weakness dictates that delivery will be, at best, episodic. Christianity is not a religion for the righteous, but for sinners. What it does require is an attempt at personal transformation. As the Saviour said to Nicodemus: you must be born again. To follow Christ is to venture into a new world – the old one, of our corruption, disappears beneath the flood. Christianity involves really hard attempts at living a good life ourselves, before we would demand decent conduct of others.

Eight

Peace on earth

ଛଠଉଓ

The message of the angels is repeated many times in the Christmas season; it is a wistful reminder that human society was made for better things than it ever manages to achieve. How realistic is it to expect peace on earth? Conflict appears to be part of the normal condition of mankind. It is not a fearful aberration of our natures, since very few occasions of conflict are actually irrational. They occur because people really do believe in their values, and seek to defend or to advance them in situations which prompt collision with competing groups. The twentieth century has been the great age of mass education and popular political participation – never before was there a time when governments were so accountable. It has also been characterized by some of the most terrifying warfare in human history.

Just as it is probably accurate to say that truth is advanced by controversy, by the testing of propositions, so it is perhaps also the case that human values are advanced by conflict. This is not a desirable situation, but it is what we have got. Violence for the achievement of moral ends may sound like a paradox, yet stripped of false pieties of expression it is what happens in practice – otherwise the twentieth century would have seen the world succumb to some horrific tyrannies. What do Christians mean, then, when they pray for peace in a worldly context which often requires war? Unless they are being absurdly naive they are praying, in effect, for a resolution of the *conditions* of conflict. That may sometimes be realistic; but what if genuinely incompatible ends are sought by the potential combatants? The

Christian course may well, in those circumstances, be support for whichever party seems most to advance the course of truth. The historical record indicates that there have been many such occasions.

The moral climate of the world is forever changing, and the aspirations of humanity are unstable. The conditions for a permanent peace will probably never exist. It is precisely because that is so that the message of the angels at the birth of the Saviour heralded a supernatural event: the normal state of human society was suspended, and the peace of God – which is a peace in the hearts of men – touched the world. The angels gathered at the grotto of Bethlehem to witness the descent of God to the earth. The miracle was not that war then ceased but that men and women were thereafter able to receive the greater peace of God into their hearts. It is the gift which the Infant Jesus still holds out, amidst the searing chaos which we have made of the world he gave us.

Nine

The year of the Lord

❧❧

At the start of the year people take stock of their lives. With the melancholy passing of time the list of things that remain unachieved tends to grow, as each of us learns to adjust the false expectations of our youth to the realities of what life can actually deliver. What do we expect of life? In modern society, alas, both Christians and non-Christians alike are liable to give priority to the pursuit of personal happiness. Ask most people what they expect of existence and that is what they come up with. Those who regard themselves as highly endowed with altruism – which is how most people see themselves – will add, of course, that happiness is what they want for other people too. It is all part of the unreflective moral sense of our age: the calculated hedonism which sustains the welfare culture.

Now if God is envisaged as the great provider of human happiness, which seems to be the assumption at the heart of popular religiosity, then a brief survey of the result of his work will show, to say the least, some deficiencies. It is no wonder that those who equate God's intentions with human contentment are among the first to lapse into unbelief. Life is not in general characterized by the provision of happiness, except for those whose perspective of reality is oblique. Similarly, religion is often conventionally regarded, even by its own practitioners, as something which is automatically pleasant and comforting – it is there to provide solace and meaning, and to confirm the warmer human sentiments. This view, too, is unsound. Religion is about the majesty of the Creator, the obligations we owe to him, the greatness of his love (which subsists in his bothering with us at all); it is about converting our time on earth into a preparation for eternity, and about the coming judgement. It is hard and demanding. It is also divisive – a feature particularly unattractive to the contemporary sense that virtually any kind of discrimination about human values is to be lamented. The parables of Jesus are about the division of mankind, into those who respond to God's calling and those who do not. It is all very precise. Nothing in his message suggests the vague universalism of modern religiosity, the benign assumption that no matter what people believe it will all be the same to God at the end of time. 'Every tree that brings not forth good fruit is hewn down, and cast into the fire,' Jesus said.

At the start of the year we might resolve to take those words seriously. That would involve abandoning the broad way of worldly happiness for the narrow path of a life which is eternal.

Ten

Easter Eve

૪૭᭨ᘓ

When Christ came to live in Nazareth time and eternity appeared together in the familiar world of our understanding. Here was the Divine in the condition of humanity. Most of his life on earth was spent undramatically in the immediate society of the Holy Family; his ministry extended for no longer perhaps than the last two years of his life. And so it is with the entire human race. By the time of the Incarnation men and women had inhabited the earth for numerous millennia. Though they were in all essentials just like us, we know almost nothing about them – a few random survivals of their artefacts are the only clues to their values or beliefs. The known story of mankind can embrace no more, in consequence, than perhaps the last five thousand years. The two thousand years that have elapsed since Christ walked the earth are hardly any length of time at all when set against the full span of human existence. Yet Christ, who on that scale is almost our contemporary, declared the impending end of time, the coming of judgement. As a flame burns brightly before it gutters and dies so the life of humanity seems now to be burning up ever more rapidly. The Lord spoke of the end as near: does that mean the next millennium, or the one after that?

In fact the end is also exactly as revealed in the life of Christ. It has in one sense already occurred, and the pivotal event was the resurrection of the Saviour. He rose, it is true, from the dead; the decisive thing, however, is that he rose to *life*. The message of Easter is new life, the rebirth of the world. The symbols we use are those of regeneration: the eggshell that needs to fracture before life begins, flowers that defy the winter cold and presage spring, the bird in flight which portrays the release of the soul from the confines of the earth. In the earliest iconography the risen Christ was depicted as a Greek youth, in the radiance of bodily vitality, before time's patina reduced him to the bearded middle-aged sage assembled in the art of the Pre-Raphaelites – and popularized by the kind of illustrations Victorians expected to see in their Bibles.

Jesus confirmed the value of the lives of the humanity that had preceded him. The Scriptures he endorsed were sacred insights of an existing tradition of understanding, and the social life he shared derived from a human pattern of organization whose existence provided space for the exploration of lasting values. But these provided, for all that, static categories. What Jesus gave was the end of the old world and the start of the kingdom – an accelerating movement of the human race which those could join who accepted his forgiveness and who regarded their time on earth as precious early instalments of eternity.

Eleven

As we forgive them that trespass

ঙ৩জ্ঞ

The recent surge of opinion about the moral state of society, initially energized by the murder of an infant on Merseyside, has amounted to something that could almost be described as a national trauma. Public debate has centred on supposedly evil individuals, on how to determine forms for the conditioning of children which are most likely to instil moral sense, on how to deal with offenders, and on the manner in which social arrangements may be adjusted to limit the occasions of lawlessness. Religion has been brought on, from the wings as it were, to witness to the importance of a moral foundation. But it is to politicians that people primarily look for a solution. Despite all the previous talk about 'rolling back the frontiers of the state', and leaving the individual free to contrive personal moral reference, people are persistent in their collectivism: it is government which must act to curb human wickedness.

Yet it is possible that the problem is not one that can be settled by politicians, nor may it be in essence moral. It is spiritual – it is about the essential nature of men and women (and children), and their unavoidable failure to attain the standards of behaviour that they can nevertheless recognize as desirable. The trouble with society today is not that it is especially liable to violent, or criminal, or merely unsocial acts, but that it has set itself a false model of what humanity itself is actually like. In this model the individual is basically benign, his actions are informed by reason; the world is, if not capable of

---

21

perfection, still able to be structured so that the prevalent optimism about the human ability to manage things may find space for expression. Mankind has become the sovereign of his environment, both material and human. When real people do not appear to act in accordance with the model, it is them and not the model which is questioned. We really cannot cope with ourselves as we actually are. So then there is a rush to locate particular 'evil' persons, or to identify the social conditions which generate delinquency.

But human wrongdoing is not because some people are particularly wicked, or even because they have failed to be taught about moral boundaries. It is because everyone is flawed in the very centre of their beings. They stand, as Christians believe, in need of redemption. It is our spiritual frailty that produces the corrupt features of our lives, and the balm for this is not our right moral conduct but God's grace. Christianity recognizes the universality of sin and of our incapacity to do anything about it ourselves. God does not give moral rectitude; he gives forgiveness.

Twelve

Community care

ജ⟨ള

Whenever the police appeal to the public for information about particular crimes – murder, or rape, or whatever – very large numbers of people inform on their neighbours, almost every one of whom, in the nature of things, must be innocent. Most crimes involving property are carried out by people within their own immediate vicinity. Victims of murder and assault are most commonly within the family of the perpetrator. Yet crime is often conventionally attributed to the breakdown of 'the community', and 'community values' are still upheld as natural social cohesives. No one is allowed to suggest that living in close-knit communities allows the concentration of hatreds, or that the community is actually the focus of brute social conformity. It is, however, arguable that the breakdown of traditional community relationships releases the individual from the thrall of custom, from the pack mentality which characterizes small-town life (and which lies just beneath the surface of urban society everywhere), and from enforced adhesion to social values which may be enormously insensitive to personal development. Choice about lifestyle, moral reference, sexual orientation, or religious belief, for example, is not encouraged by the circumstances of close community living, as observation of traditional society as it still exists in many parts of the developing world will confirm. There is a great deal of romanticism about neighbourliness in rural life and in the backstreet camaraderie of old-fashioned city districts. The reality is different. The movement of the more enterprising of the rural populations to the cities, during the industrial revolution, may have landed them in some very disagreeable slums (though they were no worse than the rural squalor from which they came) but it opened up a liberation of personal life.

Church leaders are rather given to endorsing the concept of community as the guardian of approved social values, as their emphasis, in recent years, on areas of urban deprivation indicates. It is not absolutely clear that Jesus shared their enthusiasms. For he called men and women to leave even their families for his sake; the fishermen of the lakeside left their nets. Love of God resided in the lives of those who gave up conventional human companionships: 'If anyone comes to me and does not hate his father and mother, his wife and children, his brothers and sisters – yes, even his own life – he cannot be my disciple.' In a world in which personal religious belief was itself determined by the community, Jesus called people as individuals. It would perhaps be inadvisable now to look for a return to community concepts as the way to control the symptoms of human moral frailty.

Thirteen

Community truth

ဆဌ

It is often said by Christians themselves that the Church is a 'community', but it may be questioned whether that is primarily or essentially what it is. Jesus delivered his truth, not to a set of writings or a philosophical system, but to a people. As a means of transmitting the knowledge of his presence through the centuries it was the perfect choice: people adapt to the shifting cultures of which they are a dynamic part the way ideas sometimes do not, they are capable of recognizing the developments which take place in the understanding of ideas over time, and they constitute a continuing tradition of believers which collectively has the authority to determine authentic from corrupt reinterpretations of the original message. In this great function the Church is indeed a community of those who keep the Faith. It is a community of truth. Traditional societies preserved their values through community loyalties – the Old Testament describes a people who retained their identity precisely because they successfully embodied it within the institutions of a group. In such an arrangement those who cut themselves off from this community lost their ideological identity at the same time. The world has moved forward. Partly as a legacy of nineteenth-century liberal individualism (which was in essence a secular concept), and partly through the developed interpretation of Christianity (which was taught by Christ to individuals and not to a community) we now expect people to choose religious belief for themselves. The notion of social units or entire nations collectively enforcing a religious creed offends the modern sense of personal autonomy in such matters, though to some extent we still expect the family to demonstrate internal religious uniformity.

When Christians speak of the Church as a community in today's context they do not, however, mean the perpetual unfolding of authoritative teaching through the collective guardianship of Christ's message. In general their ideal of community is a simulation of the secular world's understanding of this concept; they see the Church, in consequence, as a celebration of human qualities such as fellowship, welfare concern, justice, and so forth. Quite apart from the fact that actual church congregations may show some divergences from the ideal in that respect, it is not a very complete representation of the Church as historically received – as a celestial society, extending through time and eternity, whose seal of authority is not the transience of earthly fellowship but exact witness to closely defined religious truths. The everlasting welfare of souls depends upon it.

Fourteen

Community illusions

಄

The contemporary Christian understanding of the Church as a kind of idealized version of 'community' – a fellowship of caring, concerned people, engaged in making the world a better place – encounters a number of difficulties. Earthly communities, for example, are perhaps too imperfect a model for a company whose greater membership is already in eternity; the Church may more properly be envisaged as a society for the dissemination of truth rather than as a fellowship for immediate welfare. Actual church congregations sometimes do not inspire confidence as local agencies of a universal organization for welfare, explicitly directed by God himself, when compared with secular charities doing a much more effective and enlightened job in the same departments of human misery. The real problem with viewing the Church as a sort of sanctified community, however, is that the reasons for which men and women choose to become regular church members do not correspond to any generally agreed idea about what Christianity is.

When Jesus made assent to his teaching a responsibility of the individual rather than the community, when he established a clear relationship between the soul of each person and the Creator, he gave to humanity a gift which, as with all other gifts, could be disadvantageous if wrongly used. Individual assent to religious truth was intended to mean personal acceptance of a closely defined body of exact teaching, of doctrine. In the modern world rather the reverse now occurs. Men and women today suppose that the essence of 'sincerity' in religion is the individual manufacture of a version for oneself. A very large number of those who adhere to the Church do so because they are seeking a body which will express their individual quest for what their own emotional impulsions have indicated as 'holy'. It is a subjective set of references which are brought into play, and this is actually encouraged by a moral culture in which the *nature* of religious truth has been individualized. The message proclaimed by Christ was, on the contrary, objectively true, independent of our emotional needs: the individual was called to assent to it on his own, separately from group or community loyalties. Many who seek the satisfaction of their private enterprise religious sense within the Church are indeed looking for a body which will be essentially a promotion of caring, welfare, and community values. But it will not be authentically religious if that is all it is. Modern religious impulses are hostile to dogma, yet the religion of Jesus is about dogmatic truth. No wonder some find the Church an unsatisfying expression of their personal emotional needs.

Fifteen

The hope of sinners

ဇာလအ

Every time there is publicity about someone found guilty by the courts of a crime which society particularly abhors they are denounced as 'evil' or 'wicked' by the press – and sometimes by the trial judges themselves. In what sense should a Christian assess the guilty? It is not, for a start, always entirely clear that every crime is in fact a sin. Crimes against property were often, in the nineteenth century for example, defined by the class instincts of an unjust class society; some sexual offences of the present day may reflect ideas about human sexuality which modern research would scarcely sustain. These are areas fruitful of controversy. People also need to be clear about the moral bases of laws which could deprive them of freedom or reputation – do they depend upon Christianity for their authority, and if so, is it right that Christian morality should be compelled by the force of the state in a society of plural values? If the basis of moral law is not religious then what is it?

In the Christian understanding of the created order *all* men and women fall far short of what God created them for; the level of sin is found at around the same level in each of us – and each of us, accordingly, stands in need of God's perpetual forgiveness. In one person sinfulness may be expressed in behaviour which also happens to correspond with agreed and defined unsocial conduct: physical assault for personal gain, let us say. In another their sinfulness may yield cruelty or malice in personal relationships, which are not offences punishable by the courts. There are, for the Christian, sins of omission as well as of commission, of which the greatest, perhaps, is the human failure to use the time the Lord gives us for purposes that transcend our immediate needs. People who give in to impulses and commit crimes may be *weaker* than others but not more wicked. To the extent that some of us do not do things which we would otherwise like to do indicates, not that our essential natures are better, but that we are capable of limited resistance and so give testimony to the efficacy of punishment as deterrence. That does not, however, make us any less wicked, in the sum of our personalities. If a man lusts, Jesus says, he has committed an offence in his heart. The truth is that many people who commit crimes do so in circumstances which do not, at the time, seem to fit the model of corrupt behaviour they had learned as the moral code, and are appalled at hearing their lives categorized in the formal censoriousness of the court proceedings. Christianity is truly compassionate because truly forgiving. 'Let the one who is without fault,' Jesus said, 'cast the first stone'.

Sixteen

To seek and to save that which was lost

⅗⅗

Unseen behind the curtained partition of the quietened ward, and invisible to the agonized beneficiary, the death of a patient from an HIV-related infection is witnessed by Christ himself. Those whom the world would rather not know are always honoured thus. For the Lord came to be the hope of the outcast and the lover of the lost. A man convicted of an offence against a child is reviled by the crowd as he is escorted from the court. It is only Jesus who holds out the hand of blessing and forgiveness as he passes, unnoticed by the morally pure and the outraged upholders of decency. He is not always, perhaps not usually, wanted; Jesus is scarcely a presence to so many with whom he has, nevertheless, a relationship which is undiminished by our wrongdoing. For he is always at the door of men's hearts, ready to enter if they respond to his knock: Holman Hunt's classic icon of Christ as the Light of the World.

Christians do not take as seriously as they should the great example which Jesus gave. He came for sinners. He was accused by the moral establishment in his own day of resorting with sinners, and now, in our world, that is where he is still to be found. Those whom conventional social values isolate and reject are in reality the representatives of humanity. Their moral frailty in one dimension (or more) of their lives is matched by other failings of the respectable; it is just that some kinds of immoral behaviour attract scorn or censure where others either pass unnoticed or are not regarded as criminal or unsocial. And it is not moral failure which cuts people off from God – though never from his love which is unconditional – but spiritual neglect. Men and women do not lapse from the kingdom which Christ proclaimed because their conduct or works fall short of his demands, but because their *faith* fails. Jesus calls for amendment of life, which includes attempts at moral reformation, because an existence unstructured by his laws assists the rapid growth of weeds in the garden of the soul. Moral predictability will be of service to others, and the discipline it involves will foster self-denial in general. But moral failure will always continue, whatever our efforts, because of the corrupted natures we bear as created beings. Faith, and the treasures of spirituality, on the other hand, are a divine gift which men and women receive in spite of themselves, and they are a gift which is everlasting. So the Jesus who walked this earth in the company of prostitutes and drunkards persists, in our time, as the friend of rapists and drug-dealers. He is the sustenance of the weak – and of the strong when they, in their turn, fall.

Seventeen

Putting up with imperfection

ℬⅭℬ

Whatever the excellencies of the various humanitarian agencies and moral pressure groups who set the agenda for public concern about the state of the world, they have, in practice, two disadvantages. The first is that they exaggerate the extent or the degree of the evils they expose. Imminent disaster, massive famine, or social collapse, somehow turn out to be less catastrophic than predicted; perhaps the phenomenon of 'compassion fatigue' derives from a vague public perception that after the frenzied raising of the dust it always seems to settle down again. But no great harm done, and doubtless much good – in the enhancement of general consciousness of real human suffering. The second disadvantage is more serious. The humanitarian agencies, in the way moral reformers always do, project their various demands for action against a model which represents perfection. Governments, they are in effect saying, will fall short of approved conduct unless *every* dimension of *every* issue raised is attended to. The model is of a world purged of all imperfections – no one will be without a hospital bed at the exact moment it is needed, no single-parent family will lack the amenities which are envisaged as a universal birthright, no corner of the globe will ever experience hunger or social dislocation.

Now everyone knows that the world cannot be perfected, and each of the moral pressure groups is presumably capable of recognizing that available resources are insufficient to pay for all the benefits that are demanded. It is just that they press the exclusive urgency of their own area of concern and propaganda. Viewed from the perspectives of society as a whole, however, governments are being presented with a range of moral requirements which amount, if they could be met, to the creation of a perfect society. But they cannot be met, and even if they could our immediate successors would change the terms of engagement with the world, and new sets of demands would be made according to different models of perfection. It may be thought that it is better to aim at perfection in order to stimulate concern and then to settle for what you can get. In reality that is not the way things work. The real result is permanent dissatisfaction with government – to whom everyone seems to look for action – and the nasty pursuit of social scapegoats and moral delinquents, who are supposed guilty of creating the evils complained of.

Christians are clearly called, in the example of Jesus himself, to bind up the wounds of the afflicted and to feed the hungry. Yet they are also called to recognize that perfection is not given to men and women, nor to the world in which they live. Theirs is not to shout with anger at the state of the creation, but to labour with patience, bringing the love of God to bear upon human imperfection, until their work on earth is done.

Eighteen

Take nothing for your journey

୫୬୯୫

Just beneath the surface of modern life there is a growing problem of loneliness. It is in some sense an unavoidable consequence of the breakup of traditional society and the individualism of contemporary social culture. It is also true that people begin their passage through society with every expectation of discovering emotional security and companionship; through acquaintance with the ideals of self-development propagated by educationalists they additionally expect the enrichment both of personality and of understanding. Like the hopeless hope of losers in a *film noir* drama, or like children forever seeking more exciting video games, we persist in anticipating a life of fulfilment. What is the reality? Many of those who set out with their chosen partner to create a domestic barrier against the loneliness of existence are abruptly thrust back into it: a third of marriages fail. Increasing longevity is uneven in its effects: death of a partner leaves large numbers with an unexpected twenty years or so of life on their own – just at a time when they are least able to cope either practically or emotionally. We soon discover that the much-acclaimed self-development of contemporary education actually leaves us quite unable to put up with our self-developed minds when there is no one else around. Fine music and great art, and so forth, have a certain utility as classy entertainment, but they are no substitute for authentic spirituality or the pathos and lyricism of human love. The modern decline of belief in

---

transcendent values has meant that men and women no longer regard life on earth as a preparation for anything else; they need companionship here because otherwise there is a void.

The solution, beloved of care workers, involves the contrivance of simulations of community experience. Old people shuffled off into retirement homes by their relatives are imagined to be protected against loneliness by compulsory residence with others just as lonely. Associations and therapies are invented; hobbies are encouraged to absorb the time until the end comes. For the most truly alone of all – those trapped within relationships with others from which social convention or practical necessity will allow no escape – there is no solution. But disguising loneliness, or applying anodyne alternatives, actually does no service to the afflicted, and may, indeed, deprive them of occasions of real insight. For the truth is that human wisdom derives from detachment. Emotional isolation is a cathartic condition which presages spiritual understanding. We are alone before our Creator, and the dislocations of life can prepare us for the only enduring truth: that those for whom the world no longer seems a home are already within sight of the perimeters of eternity.

Nineteen

The human God

∞ (∞)

A lot of our difficulties about belief in God derive from a set of wrong beliefs about ourselves. Men and women today live in a kind of personal culture of entitlements. Because we have such an elevated view of what life owes us we are sceptical about the existence of a God who can allow the denial of our happiness. We are, we suppose, basically good creatures, and our lives on earth will be most adequately developed if our pursuits of contentment and security are reasonably catered for. The achievements of humanity are impressive. We have managed, in so many areas, to exploit the resources of the planet with a truly astonishing inventiveness; our art and music and literature, and so forth, bear ample testimony to the maturity and insights which have made us fit to be treated with respect and dignity. How can we believe in a God who seems to have so much less esteem for us than we have for ourselves?

The age is perhaps best characterized in the commonly used expression about the 'sanctity of human life'. It is, in fact, *so* commonly used that no one any longer pauses to consider what an extraordinary claim it presupposes. Is human life – are we – actually sacred? If we are, then we might without affront to God, perhaps, complain when life does not deliver the rich and long list of entitlements which we expect. Consider the benefits which are now regarded in the normal expectation: freedom from hunger, from illness, from social deprivation, from the accidents of existence in an unstable environment (like earthquake or flood), and from civil disorder; the rights to knowledge, understanding, equality with others, and so on. We are, as

---

we think, so good that we can only conceive of a God who is the guarantor and provider of a painless life and an assurance of personal significance for each of us.

Jesus, however, called men and women to repentance. His stark message was addressed to us as we are: self-seeking, vain, proud, corrupted by personal desires, and incapable of essential improvement through our own enterprise. Who are capable of travelling to the moon are yet moral pygmies; who create great art are spiritually frail – Leonardo da Vinci, for example, was once imprisoned for the sexual abuse of a young boy (the modern press would have called the supreme genius of Western art a 'fiend' or a 'beast'). The God we should seek to believe in is the authentic God who brings us the wholeness of his grace. Our much-vaunted achievements are dust in the balance of eternity. What we need is forgiveness.

Twenty

Window into heaven

෨෬

For many people, today will be the end of the world. Death, the unspeakable reality that haunts the fringes of modern consciousness, will for some come suddenly, and for some others as the termination of a prolonged existence fraught with pain and horror: 'man that is born of a woman hath but a short time to live, and is full of misery'. Few sentiments sit less easily with the contemporary practice of human life than this, for in modern society we do not live in anticipation either of earthly misery or of the eternity to which Christians are supposed to look as their eventual home. Life has become a scramble for personal security and material well-being, to which a cladding of cultural and aesthetic luxuriance is added as part of our seeming entitlement to the enrichment of the personality. Emotional discipline has gone; emotions are, indeed, indulged for reasons of entertainment as well as, again, in exploration of purely worldly sensation. 'As is the earthy, such are they that are earthy', as St Paul noticed. Many of the leaders of Christian opinion themselves do not appear to be greatly distanced from the prevalent culture of materialism, understanding, as some do, their religion to be a kind of sanctification of humanity's absorption with the current 'issues' of human welfare. The Christian tradition, before them, however, conveyed the ideals of self-denial, emotional austerity (St John Chrysostom said 'Christ died for our sins, and do you laugh?'), abstinence, confession of personal failings, and an interpretation of the purpose of life which emphasized its transience and imperfections. Shortly after death we are forgotten, and our time on earth is for the removal of encumbrances which keep us here. The origin of the modern inability to cope with death is to be found in a wrong attitude to life.

The word of Christian hope comes to those who are suffering a lengthy and debilitating terminal illness, or whose interior lives are bleeding with the emotional lesions of looking after loved ones who are. For Jesus did not speak of improvements to the welfare facilities of Judea, nor did he go into the desert to read great poetry or contemplate great art. His priorities were unlike ours. He sought out the simplicity of life which those who make themselves fit for eternity will always recognize. When the forces of evil offered him material solace, during the temptation in the wilderness, the Saviour pointed instead to the serenity of the spirit. The terrifying sufferings of this present time are the growing-pains of a new life; with each worldly sorrow, and with the emptiness of our attempts at understanding, the seed of the kingdom germinates more rapidly within us.

Twenty One

The poverty of
understanding

ℬ❀ℭ

Men and women once regarded themselves as strangers and
pilgrims upon the earth, a part of the general suffering and
survival of all other living things, yet also separated and raised
up by God to consciousness and reflection. They were
inseparable from the processes of creation, living out a frail
and insecure existence, never forgetful of the imminence of
personal disaster, and grateful for the considerable releases
from pain which actually came their way. Their worship of God
derived from a knowledge of this dependence. It reflected a
sense that the fragile nature of their purchase upon life
suggested gratitude, and the duty of reverence, to the divine
author of all things.

Worship is a problem for modern people, and so they tend to
convert it – when they bother with it at all – into an occasion for
emphasizing the element of human fellowship, the shared
expression of human warmth, the joy of those who have found
something which adds a measure of richness to their lives. It is
this attitude to worship which is in fact the chief indicator of a
great shift in modern understanding of religion, and it discloses
a shift, also, in modern evaluations of life itself. Men and
women no longer perceive religion to be about the duty owed
to God; it is not, any more, a response to the fearful realities of
the unseen world, to which they are eventually called in
judgement. Religion is now adopted for comparatively casual
reasons: it is understood as a 'dimension' which will provide

texture for human lives, it is considered an addition to cultural awareness, a way of giving meaning to existence and therefore of dignifying the individual – who is otherwise just a hapless excrescence of the evolutionary process. Religion, that is to say, has become human-centred, like just about everything else. Religion is not considered a duty owed to a sovereign; the concept of God's wrath, like the notion of ultimate judgement, has been relegated to the museum of antiquities. Religion is now a pleasant sensation, an emotional reassurance, reinforcing human values and human self-esteem. People shop around to find the version which will do most for them, for religion has been made to serve the ends of human happiness. Believers today are less likely to be those who surrender their unruly wills and affections in order to beg God's forgiveness: they are more likely to be the culturally articulate in pursuit of a belief system which will confirm their addiction to personal worth. But it is the fear of God which is the beginning of wisdom, and it is the great love of God which offers forgiveness even to people like us.

Twenty Two

Weeping over the city of Jerusalem

ಬಂಧ

Christian leaders today are so anxious to find evidences of religious belief in the population at large that seemingly even the most slender disposition to acknowledge the existence of non-material phenomena are greeted with approval. They recognize, it is true, some dangers inherent in aspects of, for example, New Age thinking, or in exclusivist cults which may entrap the young or vulnerable. But when it comes to cultural intimations of higher things they are markedly uncritical. Great music or art, beautiful buildings or articulations of human compassion: all are acclaimed in turn as signs of the existence of the Divine. The creativity of mankind is itself now recognized, in this humanist age, as a sort of religious enterprise. And in a way it is. For the Bible relates how men were called by God to the astonishing vocation of taking part in the development of the world entrusted to them. In their work and service they would discover the qualities which God wills as the anticipation of blessedness. The trouble is that men made weapons of mass destruction as well as wonderful art; they eat of the tree of evil as well as tilling the soil. How do we know that one act of creativity is God's work and that another is not? Outside of divine revelation there is no way. God directed men to the developments which were in accordance with his will – the Scriptures are a record of the process of divine discovery – and the coming of Christ into the world proclaimed a kingdom in which the divine imperatives were made particularly explicit.

43

Now Jesus did not direct the glances of his followers to glowing sunsets or beautiful music as the signs of the kingdom. He did not settle, as we now do, for people being somehow moved when they go into a cathedral, or acclaim virtually any elevation of the human spirit as being authentically religious. The only cathedral he spoke about at all was the temple of Jerusalem – and that was to observe that it would shortly be destroyed, as indeed it was. We need to remind ourselves that Jesus addressed himself to a people who were already religious. The Jews of his day, furthermore, were particularly well instructed in their faith, for it distinguished them from the alien conquerors who governed them. The demands of the Saviour were accordingly precise: he called for real repentance of clearly acknowledged sins, he regarded the highly articulate spirituality around him as inadequate, and his message of ethical purity required sacrifice and self-denial. Christians today, as his ambassadors in the world, should scarcely settle for vague intimations of the numinous as a substitute for the demands of their divine sovereign. Jesus calls us to the priority of personal amendment: the kingdom starts there, not with aesthetic appreciation.

———————

Twenty Three

The vocabulary of prayer

ഇൗരു

Prayer is for a Christian what training is for an athlete. Those who would achieve some insight into the nature of spirituality, and who can therefore begin to know something of the blessedness of God, must practise prayer regularly in order to foster the personal culture within which the presence of God may be recognized. Spiritual fitness increases with each attempt at prayer. But on what kind of basis or model should it be fashioned? What are the appropriate forms? In earlier religious understandings, as reflected in parts of the Old Testament for example, prayer was plainly a sanctified version of the approach a suppliant might make to an earthly sovereign. That is not to say that prayer itself was, as a consequence, earthly, since sacred and secular authority were not separated as they now are, and the honour paid to a temporal lord may indeed have been an appropriate model for constructing an approach to the eternal one. But our terms of reference today are quite different. How should we approach God? Traditional prayer comprised worship first: the sovereign was addressed through a rehearsal of his power and attributes, to which was added a list of requests, the intercessions. Modern people have difficulty with the first of these – there is nothing in our secularized understanding both of temporal authority and of religion itself which acts as a satisfactory model for verbalizing our sense of the divine sovereignty. We tend to make do instead with exclamations which simulate joy. The second element in traditional prayer is what most modern people actually call prayer: requests to God, usually concerning matters of self-interest such as health and security. These clearly raise problems of a potential conflict, between individual desires and the will of Providence, which are allowed to remain unresolved. But quite apart from that, what is lacking in the practice of prayer by so many people today is a contemplative element: listening to God, silence.

Prayer is not necessarily an emotional experience. Listening to God is frequently unaccompanied by any individual sensation of the divine presence – you don't have to feel holy. Nor is it a conjuring up of all one's finer instincts. Since prayer was taught first by Christ himself to simple fishermen it must surely follow that it is not, in essence, an affair of heavy sensibility or aesthetic accomplishment, like listening to great music. It is the emptying out of our own priorities: the true approach of the penitent to the lover of sinners. It is, above all, the gift of everyone, for the serene presence of the Saviour comes now to the most humble and broken lives as once he came to the poor and outcast of the Galilean lakeside. But without prayer you do not see him, and without penitence you do not know him.

Twenty Four

—————

The moral norms

ဆဝဪ

The public debate about the need to re-moralize the young continues to contain calls for Christianity to be more widely taught in schools and in the home. The idea is a simple one: the 'ethics of Christianity' are all about caring for others, and the result of a more effective diffusion will be a generation of young people with enhanced social discipline. As a background to this debate, which has counterparts throughout the developed world, is a general perception that the young are sinking into crime and violence because they have no stable points of moral reference. A recent American survey, for example, compared the top offences committed by students in high schools in the 1950s with the most common offences of today. For the earlier period the list began with 'chewing gum', 'making noise', 'getting out of turn in line', 'wearing improper clothing' and 'not putting paper in waste baskets'. For the present time the list began: 'rape', 'assault', 'arson', 'vandalism', 'extortion', 'drug abuse'.

This is not the appropriate place to enter the discussion about whether more effective reporting of crime accounts for a significant amount of the evident increase, nor to offer views about the raised expectations to better conduct within the general public. What is surely pertinent, on the other hand, is the seeming fact that some people are, by nature or upbringing or whatever, personally programmed to live a structured existence and some are not. The inclination to live a 'moral' life, that is to say, probably has as much to do with psychological type as it has to do with acquired codes of behaviour; just as some people who are totally without religious belief can have lives of interior serenity, and just as some who are convinced of religious truth nevertheless find themselves incapable of observing the rules of conventional morality.

Individual psychology, however, takes some of its content from the ideas people absorb early in life about right and wrong behaviour – hence the need for the teaching of a moral code. But there are severe limits to the process, which the present debate ignores.

For those who call for Christianity to be employed in re-moralizing the young the 'ethics of Christianity' are interpreted as a sort of humanism – they are a body of precepts which, if universally respected, would promote human welfare and human dignity. But it is doubtful if they would. Christianity is for people who sin and will go on sinning, because they are as they are. Here is the paradox which the moralists of our day are unable to cope with: that spiritual people are still liable to do wrong. The moral teachings of Jesus related to his kingdom; there were descriptions of how those should aspire to behave who sought to foster the personal culture in which spirituality could grow. Yet sin is not abolished from the world because people try to be good. Teaching the Christian moral laws helps people to have a reference for their lives. It does not eradicate their sinful natures.

Twenty Five

The pearl of little price

ßÓCß

The mark of the age continues to be the high estimate we have of ourselves, of our entitlements and individual worth as human beings. The worst sins we can imagine – which in a traditional understanding of religion would have related to lack of faith – are sins against humanity. The world becomes impatient of those who insist that all religions are not the same, that God makes demands which are exclusive, that religious faith itself imposes real demands that involve personal sacrifice. We prefer the bland statement that God is love, and by that we mean that God has the same high regard for us that we have for ourselves. The notion that God's love is more properly recognized in the gift of salvation, given to those whose behaviour does nothing to merit it, does not attract much belief. We do not appreciate, and so no longer widely believe in, a God whose love is eventually expressed in judgement. In modern society the concept of God, where it is entertained at all, is now likely to be interpreted as a kind of summary or collective of the human values we most wish to promote. In fact, interest in religion remains quite high, but people are usually concerned with it only as a marginal phenomenon and only as a 'dimension' which will do something for them. Hence the therapy-God, the God who is brought on to 'enrich' individual lives, to give meaning, to reinforce the sense that our self-absorption has a divine basis. Here is the instantly accessible God, whose meeting place with men is no longer the mystery of the altar but the psychiatrist's couch or the counsellor's office. God has become the servant of human need: modern men and women are returning to the crudest and earliest understanding of religion, to the childhood of the race. Religion then was simply a projection of human self-identity.

There are two unfortunate consequences of emphases and priorities like these. The first is that religion is reduced to an affair of moral concern: it is preoccupied with human relationships. Christian morality is actually the practice of spirituality in the world; the love of one's neighbour derives from the love of God. In the modern understanding of religion as morality, however, humanity itself has been deified, and religious consciousness is exhausted in human issues. Religion, that is to say, has become worldly. The second consequence is that religion is expressed as a series of 'values'. Christians themselves appear to be quite willing to do this. Religion is not recognized as concerned essentially with our spiritual natures; it is seen as a set of good attributes which give quality to human existence. 'Values', after all, are what men and women esteem, and what they most esteem is themselves. Pity the fate of this generation: their sense of religion has been absorbed by the transient anxieties of human society, and they will at the end leave the world with little enough preparation for the terrifying journey which lies before them.

Twenty Six

National crime

ೞಐ

St George: symbol of public virtue, and of the triumph of good over evil. We in England do not really make much of our patronal festival, and at the present time there is a large measure of confusion about exactly what our public virtues are supposed to be. Asked what England stands for, most politicians are likely to say 'freedom' or 'democracy'. But these are devices of government, not moral ends – what are the democratic processes and the freedoms to be used *for*? What are the previously respected moral standards which need to be restored? The public debate of recent times has assumed a plainly moral tone while simultaneously declining to identify the system of moral ideas of which it is the expression. It can hardly be the Christian religion because this is supposed to be a society of plural values; in practice public figures speak as if there is an agreed body of naturally decent ideals which can be articulated as 'human rights', shared by all people of goodwill. Along with this assertion – itself of very dubious authority – goes the assumption that there has been a moral decline, of which the 'rising tide of crime' is the symptom.

Now there has undoubtedly been an increase in crimes and in the extent to which they get reported. A lot of it, however, seems to be confined to certain areas of behaviour and to definable localities: there is a credibility gap between the media presentation of a society sinking beneath the impact of a 'crime wave' and the actual experience of ordinary people, for whom life in society appears no more hazardous than it has always been. What is equally deceptive is the perception that increased

---

crime is the consequence of personal moral decline – that children are not brought up within a moral framework. It is very likely that they really have very clear moral references, but that these are differently learned: from peer groups and media heroes rather than from the Church or the school. The role of parents is probably about the same as it has always been.

In the Christian religion there is a central adhesion to the notion that men and women are corrupted by sin, and that their essential human nature does not change. They are creatures who are flawed in the core of their being. Christians should therefore expect that the degree of immoral intention by humans will be about the same in every age and society. And so it is. What is new in our time – the 'crime wave' we observe – is simply opportunity and availability. Traditional social restraints are eroded: hence the occasions for wrong choice are greater. People now own so many material possessions: hence the rise in crimes against them. Most young people today, for all that, are morally conscious. Our moral panic, which in its popular form can be very ugly, is probably founded on insecure evidence.

Twenty Seven

———

Out of the depths

ഇൗൽ

The glamorous image of hospitals presented by television dramas, the apparently inexhaustible public preoccupation with health care, and the intrusive publicity given to the politics of medical administration, disguise the fact that hospitals are also about dying. No one really wants to think about that. Staff are anxious to emphasize that hospitals are about health rather than sickness; they also know that a ward full of people who believe they are going to survive is easy to control. Medication to diminish pain, so evidently humane, may also cloud the patient's consciousness that life is draining away, and that the time has come to prepare for the end. Relatives are commonly responsible for a well-meaning conspiracy not to tell a loved one how near they are to death – plainly quite unable to see how much that demeans the dignity of the dying, who are denied the occasion of ultimate reflection. Thus the modern inability to cope with death – a characteristic feature of a materialist culture – extends to the exclusion of a disagreeable reality: that very many people go to hospital to die. The cheery atmosphere of the light, sanitized wards actually beckons to the kingdom of death.

But the hospital is also the kingdom of Christ, the place where eternity touches the world with a celestial presence. Its wards are where Jesus witnesses the suffering of the dying, redeeming the ghastly inconsequence of individual lives with the promise of God's love; where the messy disposal of expended bodies becomes beautiful because sanctified by him; where the painful entry into eternity is the birth-pang of new life. Hospitals, properly considered, are shrines of authentic holiness: not because there is anything particularly holy about humanity and its material obsessions but because God is concerned with the fate of each life he has created. There is also, however, judgement. God gives us a space on earth in order that we shall use it to build the foundations of an eternal existence, to learn how to recognize the materials which are everlasting. Some are called from the world, in the divine Providence, without the opportunity of reflection: young children, or the victims of accidents. But most die slowly – indeed, many more than in the past, due to medical technology, and to the capacity of the body to close down by phases, sometimes over a very extended period. That provides time when people should be told that their end is impending, so they can put their lives in order. The hospital ward is luminous with the presence of the Saviour, inviting those who love him to a splendour which exists even amidst the fearful squalor of decay.

Twenty Eight

The kingdom of God

ೲೲ

There seems to be an almost universal inclination to imagine the existence of an ideal place, a perfect society, a realm free of suffering and decay. Sometimes it is purely a country of the mind, an interior solace against the unsatisfactory nature of an individual life. Sometimes it is a wistful fantasy, not really believed in, but somehow conveying a serene vision of the world as it ought to be: a land of plenty, or of complete harmony where the wolf and the lamb feed together. It is the perfect kingdom, over the rainbow; it is where the hopeless dreams of losers rather movingly come true. To the people of the ancient world it was a time yet more ancient – the golden age, a first Arcadia, from which the terrifying forces of primordial chaos were excluded by the sovereignty of virtue or the benign permission of the gods. Today's version is fostered by the ecological movement, with its projection of a pure world unsullied by the activities of human society; an updated Romantic landscape, in which men and women discover ideal relationships in a natural environment from which the serpent of pollution has been banished. The Utopia, the Golden Age, the Land of Oz: humanity at its most vulnerable regards the horrific facts of life on earth and endeavours to replace them with an imagined but unattainable perfection. To this category should be added the modern perception of heaven – not as the domain of judgement and divine will, but as a kind of ideal earth, somewhere beyond sight, where the unsatisfactory relationships of the present are transformed, where love reigns, where there is no sickness, and where everyone is happy.

For Christians, however, the kingdom of heaven is not a golden utopia but the actual world of our experience. The kingdom of Christ is the real world, and those who try to pattern their lives upon the most perfect life of Jesus are its inhabitants. This is where the materials of spirituality are to be found, and where the individual soul fashions its eternal existence – here and now, this side of death. Spiritual formation is about creating, in ourselves, the citizenship of the everlasting country, not of the imagination, but of the divine truth, founded upon the realities revealed by Christ. As creatures of the earth we can only know about eternal values in earthly and in human terms. That is why the kingdom that is everlasting actually begins with the empty marriage, the ungrateful child, the disappointed hopes; its landscape is the cancer ward, the carnage of the battlefield, the prison cell of those who cannot match society's demands. The kingdom does not assemble itself, and it is not derived from the degrading pursuit of personal happiness. Its existence is in the heart of the AIDS patient and the refugee; all those whom Jesus calls his own, and who respond by using the precious gift of time to create the means of recognizing eternity.

Twenty Nine

They know not what they do

ℰ✦ℭ

Fewer and fewer young people in this country are able to recite the Lord's Prayer by heart. Among the reasons why this is to be lamented is that they are not, in consequence, acquainted with one of its central statements: God is asked to forgive sins 'as we forgive those who sin against us'. It cannot be said that older people, either, despite their presumed knowledge of the prayer, set a good example of forgiveness. Indeed, the television screens are these days often filled with the victims of crime, or their relatives, calling for longer sentences than the courts have given to offenders. It is an example of emotional force which once would have been described as revenge, but which is legitimized in today's social language. The unforgiving victims always say that their motives are altruistic – that they don't want others to suffer as they have suffered.

Now crime, particularly crime against the person, can be deeply disturbing; the whole personality seems violated and a terrible sense of insecurity may result. Lives are ruined by the wicked acts of others. There exists, on the other hand, a growing capacity for emotional self-indulgence in modern society, and an inability to cope with life's misfortunes whether they are trivial or gross. It was once considered a test of moral character that the individual could absorb life's shocks and show a degree of resilience; it was a mark of maturity, an acceptance that in the world as it is (rather than as we would like it to be) there is tribulation. In today's society, with personal happiness as its goal, virtually anything that impedes individual contentment is perceived as an enormous injustice. The religion of Jesus is the religion of forgiveness. Christ swept away the legal structure of the old Jewish religion, with its tariff of retributive justice, its eye for an eye, its division of mankind into the righteous and the unclean. He came, as he said very explicitly, not for the righteous but for sinners. As he forgives, so should we: it is the core of the Saviour's message that the universality of sin should presage universal forgiveness. And that is extremely hard, since it goes against our natures. Revenge is always so easily represented as justice. There is a legitimate element of deterrence in the practice of justice, but this, too, can readily be corrupted by emotional outrage. Some of the recent baying for harsher punishments, which has accompanied the debate about crime, darkly suggests a primitive layer of human nature just beneath the surface of modern life. But the world is made new at Whitsun; it is the birthday of the Church. Now is the time to remind ourselves that Christianity is costly: the believer has to renounce some of his most basic human instincts in order to forgive others their trespasses.

Thirty

The Trinity of love

ℬℭ

The lonely and the unloved are loved by Jesus; the wicked and the corrupted are loved by him too. The Saviour illuminates the darkest lives with his presence, for the religion of forgiveness can be received by all who respond to the calling of Christ. When the young feel rejected by the world they are likely to become victims of histrionic self-indulgence, taking a short-term view in a situation which requires a long-term perspective, acting with limited experience of life. But when the old feel rejected they are likely to be right. For them the possibilities have come to an end, the opportunities for development have closed up, and the assessment of future change is necessarily abbreviated. The human sensation of being cornered by circumstance, boxed in through an arrangement of things, which is common enough throughout life, becomes, for the old, a very pressing reality as the sands of time slip away.

The wise person, however, is the one who is actually indifferent as to whether the world needs him or not. For wisdom resides in creating a world in oneself. It is fitting out an interior life as one might prepare a ship for a voyage or an aircraft for a flight: this is the purpose of spiritual formation – of establishing self-sufficiency in everything that needs to survive our brief experience of the earth. It is, in its nature, a lonely undertaking, since only the individual can prepare himself for personal survival. Earthly companionships and love, through which we discover so much of the texture of our spiritual beings, are nevertheless transient; they are destined to fall away, and only the fragrant memories endure. We devise means to domesticate the planet and seek anodynes against the stark truth of our loneliness. But in the end there is just the individual person, placed in judgement before God. Then all that is left is the interior life, the spiritual creature.

The Christian religion brings to this fearful depiction a quite startlingly supportive dimension – no less than the whole panoply of heaven, the eternal companionship of the saints, the supreme friendship of Jesus. To assent to Christ is to join an immense spiritual society, most of whose members do not exist in the world of our present senses. It used once to be believed by the early Church, and is by many still, that as the priest celebrates the Holy Eucharist he is invisibly surrounded at the altar by angels, who gather to witness the return of Christ to the world. And so it is with individual lives; they are joined by an eternal host whose spiritual loveliness transcends the confines of personal loneliness. That is the promise of Christ, guaranteed by the gift of the Holy Spirit – who will keep us, as the Lord said, in all truth.

Thirty One

Marching as to war

ಏಂಡಿ

The breakup of traditional society and the individualizing of moral values, with the consequent advantages and disadvantages, does mean that ideas and institutions which we wish to succeed in the modern world will have to work with different tools. Religion must no longer look either to the family or to public provision for its propagation. How, then, do values get disseminated in our day? Despite the conditioning given to their children by parents, and the enormous influence allowed to schoolteachers in the classroom, the fact is surely that ideas and cultural norms are now passed on by the media – and principally by television. Now the media arena is an active and volatile place; ideals and ideologies which are to succeed need to battle for space. They have to go on the ideological offensive. In our own century Fascism succeeded by attacking race enemies, Communism by attacking class enemies, nationalism by attacking colonialists and cultural enemies. What are the Christian Churches attacking?

The first answer is that they should be attacking sin. No one, however, listening to the rhetoric that proceeds from the Churches today, could receive an impression that they are calling for individual repentance. The popular message is that God is love, and loves indiscriminately; we do not want to know about a God who judges, and the prevalence of humanism precludes the possibility of representing men and women as corrupted and debased. The next enemy that Christianity might be expected to attack is false religion – the other world religions, after all, show little enough respect for Christianity in the countries where they have ascendancy. But other religions are today treated with great respect, and a natural disinclination to get involved with criticizing the beliefs of non-European peoples restrains Christian leaders from going on the assault here. Those other religions, furthermore, are packaged in a very sanitized way for presentation in Western societies – often very different from the actual practices of the cultures in which they are rooted. Christianity should, above all, attack the greatest threat to mankind today: materialism, the interpretation of men and women as creatures of circumstance, their transcendence denied. That, in its popularized form, is the basis of most views of human life that are now current in educated society, stronger and more effective in Western liberal societies – because rarely identified – than ever they were in Communist states with their frank atheism.

For no theatre of ideological warfare is modern Christianity actually prepared, however. There is, within the leadership, a horror of controversy and a distrust of those who rock the boat – who show, that is to say, ideological precision. Thank God that Jesus died for our sins, and did not attempt, as we evidently might, to arrange a compromise solution to human sin.

Thirty Two

The value of time

෨ଓଓ

In modern society the distinction between fantasy and reality is routinely blurred. Throughout the centuries of human history the lives of individual men and women have been very thinly textured: their areas of experience have been narrow, localized, emotionally confined; the data upon which they have been socialized has been patchy. The life of man upon the planet, that is to say, has been poor and his expectations have, correspondingly, been rather low. That has now all changed, and with a rapidity that – had mankind not been so adaptable – might well have produced social breakdown. What it has produced is considerable social diversity. Consider the lives of people in Western society today. Education has heightened personal expectations; mobility and the free availability of information have destroyed authentic local identity; the leisure revolution and the manipulation of emotions by daily exposure to entertainment on the television screen have opened a whole new territory of vicarious experience; increased wealth has resulted in personal ownership of an enormous range of goods and products which would have astonished our ancestors. Each one of us, through television, is transported to different cultures every day; we acquire instant opinions on public affairs; we move through time at the shift of programme scheduling, from a historical drama to a documentary about the dinosaurs.

In the now classic film by Alain Resnais, *Last Year in Marienbad*, the sequences of past and present are so mixed up that the notion of time itself is relativized. The whole of life in society is now becoming like that. But our daily exposure to a chaotic assemblage of information and images actually gives us the opportunity – which we do not take – to detect an important spiritual truth. It is that our lives in the world are only a fraction of our total existence in eternity, and that the rapid switches of mood and image which the modern world imposes on us may really help us to envisage something of the nature of eternity. By relativizing time we are able to see ourselves in a larger context than life in limited and localized circumstances allowed to our predecessors. What we should experience, amidst this kaleidoscope of information and entertainment, is disorientation. Therein lies the potential for spiritual growth. We are offered the chance to see that the values of the world are unstable, and that we receive them, anyway, through the manipulative presentation of others – and that our spiritual natures belong in another world altogether. But in practice we postpone eternity, seeing it as something of the future rather than as beginning here, in individual lives, as men and women recognize the fragmentary and unsatisfactory manner of our acquaintance with reality. The information revolution has not liberated us; it has, on the contrary, confirmed our absorption with the world.

Thirty Three

Faith which is truth

ဆာ‍ငာ

The English people are astonishingly ignorant about the doctrines and principles of Christianity. It is not an ignorance restricted to the less educated, furthermore, and the terrifying truth is that many who reject the Christian faith do so without any real idea of its true nature. It comes as a considerable surprise to those teaching university students, for example, to discover that after a decade and a half of being instructed in schools which have a legal obligation to provide religious education most students are quite unaware both of the history of the Church and of the teaching of Christ. They have, as has society in general, a vaguely defined moralism, which they identify with core Christianity, and adhere it unhesitatingly to whatever else attracts their moral enthusiasm or their respect for humanity. Very many people in our society, to give another example, happily combine a belief in reincarnation, which they seem to find a spiritually beautiful idea, with the Christian religion. But the two are fundamentally incompatible since Christ was emphatic that each individual life is followed by final judgement. There exists in this country a species of folk religion whose content varies from person to person. One wonders how much of its content is stable or lasting: souls are lost at an enormous rate, and the merciful invitation of Christ is not even recognized, let alone accepted.

The Church is responsible for the Christianization of England, and after centuries of endeavour it seems to have left a thin enough spiritual culture upon the national landscape. In some societies, and particularly those in which Orthodoxy and

Catholicism and biblical Protestantism are strong, people are so well instructed in Christian truth, even today, that when they lapse from regular Christian worship the surviving deposit of Christianity in the texture of their thought is recoverable later in life, or at death. In England, by contrast, there is almost nothing. When people here observe what they think of as evidence of an enduring Christian inheritance they are actually looking at institutions, like Christian schools or colleges, which were originally founded by groups within the former governing classes as the vehicle of their moral seriousness.

The popular folk religion of England is really just pagan superstition expressed in the symbolism and iconography of Christianity. It has no activist basis and no doctrinal content. Jesus, however, had very precise requirements for those who would follow him: they must make a decisive change in their lives (their moral behaviour) but also, and supremely, in their beliefs (their spiritual formation). What we tend to do is to fashion a religion for ourselves as individuals. What he demands of us is that we should surrender to his sovereignty.

Thirty Four

Faith which is demanding

⍧⍧⍧

Everybody acknowledges that the practice of humility is part of the Christian vocation. What is less evident is that humility is not some kind of metaphor or ideal: it was actually intended by Christ that we should all put it into effect in our own lives. The Lord himself gave the supreme example. God became man, the eternal sovereign became subject to the laws of his own creation, and suffered the humiliating agony of death upon the cross. Nothing that we do can match that sacrifice. In reality, however, the circumstances of life in modern society, with its success-orientated work ethic, and its inclination to evaluate achievement in material terms, does little to encourage even the first steps in the practice of humility. A life which is intended to be sacrificial; a life dedicated to the service of others because in that way Christ himself is served – is a life which really will be characterized by personal disadvantage. The brutal truth is that those who promote themselves, who are self-publicists, are the ones who come to occupy positions of power and influence, and those who try to be humble end up at the bottom of the stack if they are truly effective at it. Humility is achieved at high cost. It can mean a life which to the world's judgement may appear unsuccessful; it can also mean the loss of self-esteem through the dispiriting fact of marginalization. Humility is conventionally praised in our culture and almost universally not practised. We are, nevertheless, called to be fools for Christ's sake, and turning down personal advantage and worldly advancement as a dimension of spiritual formation will inevitably look foolish.

Humility also means accurate self-assessment. It will certainly be the case in many lives that success is not attainable anyway, because personal qualities or behaviour in social relationships are unsuited to desired goals. Humility in these cases is not voluntary self-sacrifice but a recognition of individual deficiency: that is just as hard, and as rarely practised. The world is full of people whose bitterness derives from a false evaluation of their own entitlements.

The way of discipleship is a hard way. We never quite appreciate how hard. The Lord whom we seek to serve comes fortunately into every imperfect life; he does not demand that we are achievers – but that we set our feet upon the path of endeavour. The loveliness of his presence obliterates the ugliness of our self-seeking, and our failings are forgiven in his mercy. 'For whoever will save his life shall lose it,' he tells us; 'and whoever will lose his life for my sake shall find it.'

Thirty Five

The wonderful and great mystery

ಬಂಞ

Christians today do not take as serious a view of the Church as they should. Some regard it as a kind of social consequence of claiming a Christian belief, as if the Church, in a defining statement, is a collective of warm human fellowship. The purpose of the Church, in such a perspective, is then judged by what it does for individual adherents – how it comforts them, gives them a sense of personal significance, elevates their pursuit of material welfare, or cultivates a sense of beauty or fulfilment. For some others, the Church is to be dismissed precisely because it has failed to deliver these perceived benefits; then it is the corruption and human failings of the Christians who have constituted the Church over the centuries which are highlighted. There are those who, parodying the ethicists of the nineteenth century, see the Church as having failed to follow the vision of Christ himself: they contrast the great moral teacher with the authority structure and power of the actual Church of history. But it is the first point which is the most decisive. People are dismissive of the Church when it fails to do anything to satisfy their expectations of it, and their expectations, as it happens, are not usually in correspondence with the purpose for which the Church exists.

For the Church is not just a local assembly of well-intentioned people, nor is it a place for emotional exchange or social therapy. It is, as it has always proclaimed itself to be, a mystery: the infinite and eternal truths are entrusted to the keeping and transmission of simple men and women. When God came into the world in Christ, and offered humanity a perfect representation of ultimate truths, it was a sublime moment in a process of development. God had before that shown his presence in the materials of his creation; he had revealed himself in a religious tradition. In Christ he brought mankind forgiveness and salvation – but the historical and material processes did not stop.

God entered a world of values and cultures which is, in the economy of his providence, forever changing. Christ, as part of the process, did not commit his truth to static moments of the shifting culture – he did not write a book or set up a philosophical system. He committed himself and his eternal message to the very agents of change: to men and women. He gathered the apostles, he sent out the seventy; before his serene departure from the world he instructed those who loved him to teach his truth to all nations. The Church is his body in the world. The Church is not a random assemblage of individuals in pursuit of personal meaning or fulfilment but the mysterious presence of the Saviour, protected in the essentials of the faith by the Holy Spirit, and charged with handing on the knowledge of God to all people for all time.

Thirty Six

Dust before the wind

ॐ

Why should I belong to the Church? It is surely possible to be a
good Christian without going to church? These questions are
often asked, and understandably so. In the modern world, after
all, information is readily available; people can now get some
kind of understanding of Christianity through general education, or from retrieval systems, in ways which were not
available to those who lived in the highly localized circumstances of traditional society. There was also an entertainment
element in the religion of the former world which the leisure
revolution of our own day has obliterated forever. The
emotional sustenance once provided by religion has modern
substitutes, in the various aesthetic sensations derived from the
arts and from popular music. The impulse of social service
experienced by moralists, seemingly compulsively – once the
monopoly of the Church – is now catered for by the secular
medical and welfare industries: the hero of contemporary
culture is not the priest in the slums but the doctor on the
hospital ward. The spread and quality of education promotes
the conviction that mature people can arrive at religious truth,
should they feel the need, without any resort to the Church.

But it is illusory to suppose that the Church can be so easily
dispensed with, and it anyway rests on an imperfect notion of
what the Church actually is. We live on borrowed time. The
information now available about Christianity is due to a large
favourable balance laid up by the faithful in the past. If we do
not add to it, or take active measures to preserve it, those who
come after us will face spiritual destitution. The modern wealth

71

of information, furthermore, is not as rich as it looks. Technology and educational enterprise have provided the *means* of conveying ideas – they are the mechanics, no more. The ideas themselves, the concepts being conveyed, require constant study and adjustment; like living things they need to be nourished or they will languish. The Church is the body of Christ in the world, the means by which he is conveyed to each society and culture. The Church is not a holy club or a pleasant local dispensary of spiritual consolation, but the means of preserving and enriching the knowledge of God. To be a Christian is to be part of Christ's body: it is not a mere option for those who seek belief – it is an essential. After the primary duty of personal salvation comes the salvation of others, and that unavoidably involves the corporate witness of the Church. Communities of believers may show all the irritating characteristics of humanity; they may be given to all kinds of corruption and worldliness. Yet for the Christian to adhere to the Church is a duty, for it is to love Christ's body, to be united to his everlasting presence.

Thirty Seven

For all the saints

ଈୠ୦ଔ

The Christian Church which we see and have opinions about is only a fraction of the whole. This next week the Church celebrates the festival of All Saints, and it reminds us that most of the members of Christ's body are not in the world at all, but have passed, through death, into the greater part of the kingdom. The entire Church comprises all those who have preceded us in the Christian life, who in their lives on earth preserved the teaching of the Saviour and handed it on to us, and who now, in God's providence, are with the celestial society awaiting, also like us, the end of time itself. That everlasting Church is invisibly present; its prayers sustain the living, and its existence links the world of our present understanding to the mystery of eternity. Knowledge of the truth of Christianity, fortunately, does not depend upon those of us who are in the physical world, but on this wider and larger company. Those who would judge the Church should look to this timeless society rather than to the weaknesses and ambiguities of those of us who are still on earth.

It is also in this perspective that the Church may properly be seen as the consolation of the distressed, the home of the homeless. It is quite possible, in the world, for those who seek consolation in the actual churches of their experience to find little that seems conducive. The characteristics of our humanity do not diminish because we aspire to be the agents of Christ's message, and members of the Church in the world may well disappoint or prove a stumbling-block. But the whole Church, that greater assembly of those who have tried to love God, the invisible family, the saints, are a source of authentic consolation. For in the world there is loneliness and personal desolation of spirit, and a harrowing sense of loss. Men and women try sadly to recover something of the camaraderie and affections of their earliest friendships and loves, when the world seemed simpler and the future limitless. Like those who remember childhood friendships in Rob Reiner's film *Stand by Me*, they seek to recapture, in later years, that sense of belonging, the idealized relationships and loyalties of a golden past. It is never possible to do so; time moves on, and all things change. The Church of Christ, however, joins the past and the future – it is both present and invisible. The Church, furthermore, is intended by its nature to be the refuge of sinners, the home of the lonely, the friend of those who have no one. All the saints extend their embrace across the mystery of death: their everlasting welcome offers serenity to those who are troubled by the collapsed hopes of earthly life.

Thirty Eight

The sheepfold of truth

ଶ୦ଓଽ

As the body of Christ in the world the Church extends his love to the whole of humanity; it is a welcome to the household of the Lord, to be part of the great company of believers. Because the natures of men and women are inseparable from their circumstance, and are moulded by the accidents of time and culture, the members of the Church necessarily get caught up in the moral preferences and moral failings of the world around them. At certain times they will reflect insensitivities, or promote wrong views about how people are or should behave. Protected in truth about the nature of God by the Holy Spirit the Church never departs from an authentic declaration of essential doctrine, but when it comes to moral conduct in the society of men, or what constitutes moral sin, there will always be a mixture of the earthly with the divine insights. These deficiencies, however, affect the members of the Church who are in the world at any given moment; the whole Church, the wider company of all those in eternity, press near to the earth to extend the love of Jesus to those who seek it. For the Church of Christ is the possession of the unloved and the despised; it exists for the inadequate or the desolate of spirit, the lonely, the sinful, and the morally impure. Incorporated within its membership are all those who try to love God, and whose humanity calls out to the author of all things – from the drag queens in Soho to the wives of solicitors in Surbiton. The Church is the place where the divine love meets the agony and the exultation of the living, and where Christ reigns over a kingdom that is intended even for those whose lives do not correspond with the demands of the moralists. 'For he considered that they were but flesh: and that they were even a wind that passeth away, and cometh not again' (Psalm 78 v. 40).

In the evanescent landscape of Galilee – which in our post-Romantic culture seems beautiful, but which in the ancient world was a place of labour, the inspiration of the parables – the Saviour proclaimed the universal love of God. His body on earth still proclaims it. The earliest images of Christ, following his own words, were those of a shepherd: murals in the catacombs of Rome show him as a Greek youth holding a pastoral staff. To be in the sheepfold of the Saviour is to be protected in all truth and incorporated into his love. In the world, it is to be part of his body. And the astonishing fact is that no one is better qualified than anyone else for this: Jesus accepts all who listen to his words and try to obey them.

Thirty Nine

Called to our lower natures

☜☞

The Church witnesses to the transcendence of man; that he is
made of the dust of the earth, that he derives his understanding
of things from the mechanics of the material creation, and yet
is destined for more than earthly life.

It seems an oddly commonplace thing to have to point out.
But a great deal of scepticism about religion in the modern
world is caused by the demand that life should be free of pain
and insecurity. How is it possible to believe in a God, people
ask, who allows suffering? If men and women were merely
material creatures the question might have some limited
pertinence: God could have arranged a world in which virtually
all the conditions which produce human nobility and creativity
would not exist. These are things like tragedy, heroism,
sacrifice, loyalty, the demands of love, the hope of a better
order, the pursuit of truth – all conditions which are
immediately related to human experience of pain and
insecurity. Our culture is derived from them. A world without
them, a world which provided unbroken happiness – a world
such as modern people seem to expect God to have made –
would be devoid of higher thought and finer sentiment. It
would lack the experiences which lift humanity from the rest of
the creation; which make men and women reflective beings
and candidates for eternity.

The depth of modern materialism can be recognized in the
demand for permanent happiness. When God is dethroned,

humanity and its needs become the centre of all things. Hence the obsession with welfare in our day. The icons of our society are now the medical institutions, the aid agencies and charities, the emergency services, and so forth. The physical comfort and security of the individual is regarded as hugely more important than his ultimate beliefs and values: we have come to think that the material welfare of mankind, and standards of living, should have priority over ideology or religion. This actually emerged rather clearly at the population conference organized by the United Nations in Cairo this year. The mechanics of population control were allowed to achieve a large ascendancy over the morality of individual practice. This is not to say that the advocates of population control were wrong in their objectives, but that they acted in a substantially materialist frame of reference. It is a chilling picture of the future of mankind: a species destined for transcendence but opting for material security. People cannot believe in a God who has so much less regard for personal welfare than they have themselves. The greatness of God's love was not that he eliminated human suffering – the very means of self-discovery – but that Christ died to redeem us.

Forty

The end of the year

ঙ১প্র

The Church is the only institution in the world which exists simultaneously in time and out of it. Its membership links the world with the celestial society, and to belong within the sheepfold of Christ is to receive not only the guarantee of his truth but also the unseen companionship of the blessed. In the modern world we tend to regard time, like just about everything else, as a commodity: we want more of it, are outraged when an individual life is short, endlessly seek ways of prolonging our existence, and eventually end our time in a series of lonely diversions until death. Men and women, that is to say, spend much of their time on earth seeking ways of extending lives whose purpose increasingly escapes them; a paradox obviously related to the decay of religious belief. Time brings change in all things, and above all in ourselves. The wise person will recognize that it is impossible to separate an individual life from the perpetual transformation of everything else, and will accordingly look for some means of distinguishing what is good in particular sequences of change from what is liable to corrupt truths received from the past. We are called to be in a state of permanent adaptation, and to regard time, not as a mere commodity, but as the vehicle of wisdom, the gateway of the heavenly city.

Our Saviour said a lot about time. The days, he proclaimed, were evil, and the faithlessness of the world was ushering mankind into a fearful judgement. Before the end, therefore, there must be personal identification of sin and an act of repentance. We do not know– as those who first heard him did not know, either – whether humanity is in its infancy or is already nearing the cataclysmic occurrences which will portend judgement. But Christ told them, and us, to take no thought for the urgent worries of the world and to seek out the everlasting values, the pearl of great price. We have already lost what he emphasized so clearly: that we should regard transience as the natural state of all things, that the passing of time is not to be lamented but seen for what it is – the enhancement of our proximity to God. 'For he knoweth whereof we are made: he remembereth that we are but dust,' Psalm 103 declares; 'The days of man are but as grass: for he flourisheth as a flower of the field. For as soon as the wind goeth over it, it is gone: and the place thereof shall know it no more.' As the year ends, and human society hurtles into a new division of time, we should pause to recapture the elegiac beauty of our transience. We shall not, either individually or as a race, be here for ever.

Forty One

False priorities

૪૭જી

It is depressing to hear the reasons people give for their political preferences. 'They are not doing anything for me'; 'I don't see how I shall be better off with them in government'; 'why is more not being spent so that I can have more benefits?' It is the common discourse of the street television interview or the bar exchange. After four thousand years of civilization the highest ideals which people can imagine are centred in a discussion of the relative merits in alternative systems of material welfare. Instead of people asking how the organization of the state can symbolize higher human aspirations, and so encourage the finer rather than the baser natures of mankind, they now seem content to ask what is in it for them. The leaders of opinion, furthermore, seem to encourage the view that it is human material welfare itself which is the highest moral good to which society can aspire. The debate about Europe shows up our situation well: it is not about the concept of a cultural identity, a shared religious tradition, or the style of political structures which reflect and maintain them: it is all about the economic devices which will most benefit the people of this country. The treatment of the Ulster Unionists is another indication. Here is a surviving pocket, inside the United Kingdom itself, of people who really do associate their political, cultural and religious values with the organization of the state. They are as a result regarded, by English liberal opinion, as 'sectarian'. The English political classes talk, instead, about the need for Ulster opinion to be formed not by ideas but by the familiar priorities of peace and security. It is fundamentalist materialism – regarding material welfare as more important than the ideas for which people exist.

The same sense that results in the public evaluating politics in terms of individual advantage also, alas, conditions their attitude to religion: 'What's in it for me?' Christianity is now reduced to a kind of sanctified feel-good condition, in which individuals experience an entitlement to a whole range of emotional satisfaction. Religion is actually about the sovereign commands of God, and about the duty of believers, once assent has been voluntarily given, to obey. It is not intended to obliterate the sorrows of life, nor to make people permanently happy: it does not owe anyone an intellectual explanation of the world, and it is not even necessarily nice. The last point is important. Because religion is about the obligation we owe to God it involves a high incidence of self-denial; it goes against the grain of our human inclination: we place personal security above personal sacrifice. The profession of Christianity is something the individual has first to learn and then to work at. There is a spiritual beauty attaching to the heroic endeavours which thus become inseparable from even the humblest lives, and a dignity in those who regard the gift of life as conditional and demanding. Like the righteous man who went into the Temple to pray, the materialists have their reward, in a measure of worldly security. It is the sinner who admits his sin, however; whose citizenship is in eternity.

Forty Two

———

Easter renewal

ﻼﻼ

The schemes proposed by humanity for the renewal of the
world are thick across the historical record. It is a purified earth
that is envisaged by the ecologists; a place purged of the stains
of human recklessness, a return to some imagined time of
innocence when men and women somehow lived in a natural
relationship with their environment. Economists propose
security: this or that mechanism will promote the growth of
activity, and the consequent enrichment of society will
enhance the quality of life and diminish the chance of
misfortune. The structural changes laid out by politicians also
promise security – their new world, however, is additionally
going to achieve justice and peace. Humanity never seems to
learn the ancient lesson that the heavenly cities built on earth
always come tumbling to the ground, and that the new cities
fashioned out of the rubble end up just like their predecessors.
The twentieth century has been the great age of the secular
enlightenment. Our plans for the world, we have calculated, are
based on real data and reliable scientific knowledge. Yet
twentieth-century essays in world renewal – and there have
been many of them, on a mass scale – have all, so far, ended up
like the earlier ones. To some extent, it is true, men and women
themselves keep moving the goal posts. No sooner is one
desired change achieved than they all start calling for something else, and one generation's panacea becomes another's
problem – the ecologists have discovered this as they ruefully
contemplate the mess left by yesterday's rise in living
standards. The wise, however, have always seen that humanity

is not in control. They also know that there is no age of innocence in men's past to which a return can be made, that the planet is permanently in something of a human crisis, and that the expectations of men and women are not capable of fulfilment.

Christians know that Easter is the authentic renewal of the world. For them the triumph of Christ over death signals a new creation; it is not a new world which results, however, and neither humanity nor the structures of life are changed. It is we as individuals who are changed. Not in our personalities but in our spiritual natures. Men and women are themselves the materials of the new creation. Christ descends to the earth and is with everyone, whether they acknowledge his presence or not. The supreme disposer of the universe – this is the miracle of the Christian faith – is serenely present among his creation, renewing lives which, in worldly terms, seem irredeemable. We never take seriously the truly radical effect of Christ's presence: the world itself is illuminated by the celestial forces, and the least of God's children are made citizens of eternity. The schemes of the ecologists and the economists and the politicians have only fleeting significance; the new life of salvation is everlasting. The structures of the world remain, and men and women remain conditioned by them. But their spiritual beings are transformed, for the people that walked in darkness have seen a great light.

Forty Three

Where is thy sting?

ක‍ර‍ග

The death of Christ has sanctified death. It can have, or should have, no terrors beyond the natural fears which are inseparable from contemplation of the unknown world to which we are beckoned. Modern people, however, are unable to cope with death, and when they encounter it, through the demise even of someone they hardly know, they tend to dramatize both death itself and the effect of its chilling presence upon the survivors. The culture of the day tends to sanitize death, or to celebrate the merely human qualities of the deceased rather than to envisage, in any realistic manner, the possible effects of impending judgement. We don't like to think of judgement at all, in fact, despite the emphasis given to it in so many of the parables of Christ. Just as the pagans were buried with their favourite possessions, and with the necessities to assist their journey in the afterlife, so in the neo-paganism of the modern world death rites are centred on the humanity of the departed instead of on the spiritual odyssey which is the actual purpose of life. It is now routinely expected that the funeral rites of the dead will include recordings of favourite songs, or recitations of poetry, which the dead person liked: it is as if the pagan grave goods have been replaced by the compact disc. The traditional funeral rites of the Church, in contrast, set the life of man starkly into the general context of the ephemeral nature of all things – they are a commemoration, not of the human accidents of the departed, but of the everlasting changelessness of God and of the transience of human existence.

Why do people dramatize death so much? They could cope

with it much better in former societies, perhaps because it was more familiar. Most people today have never seen a corpse until they are mature adults. But in a Christian church the corpse of Christ hangs upon a cross, everlastingly sacrificed for our sins; the very thing we most seem to fear is at the centre of our religion. Modern people have converted life itself into a scramble for security and comfort: no wonder they are terrified at the mocking capacity of death to destroy their priorities in an instant. Do they really want to live forever? Presumably not, for it is an irrational idea – if there was no death all living things would go on forever, the planet would long since have choked on itself, and without the perpetual renewal of life, ideas and values themselves would have become stagnant. So death is essential for life, and the death of Christ, celebrated this Eastertide, converts that life into eternal life. This is the beauty of transience, the melancholy truth that we are all of us brothers and sisters of the rest of creation, mutually dependent for sustenance, locked together in a chain of recycling until the end of the world. Our individual insignificance in the perpetual process is redeemed by Christ. But first we need to use our lives to know him.

Forty Four

The spiritual
adventurers

ℬℭ

It is often said that there is a renewed interest in the spiritual in
our day. To what extent is that really the case? There is certainly
a sense in which people are increasingly dissatisfied with the
circumstances of modern living and of what they are getting
out of it, and seek another dimension to their lives. Some then
try to find a meanings system – a body of ideas which explains
the whole of existence and the place of the individual within it,
and which is internally consistent so that the issues which have
troubled great minds through the ages are finally settled. In
religious terms this generally results in a New Age style of
belief, or in a philosophical construct which relates all
phenomena to a single purpose. Others, however, prefer to
opt for a self-made spiritual consciousness in which the
individual achieves serenity and emotional peace. This solution
is likely to be touched with aesthetic sensibility, and it also
suggests a great preoccupation with personal yearning for
cosmic significance. Here the pursuit of the spiritual is heavily
dependent on fashions of thought and on what people who
'think for themselves' are supposed to be thinking. There are
also social class overtones: there are more seekers after spiritual
novelties within the articulate sections of the bourgeoisie than
there are elsewhere – though the point should not be laboured,
since the popular television presentation of virtually any
religious positions (apart from the historic and conventional
creeds) encourages people of all sorts to become active in

private enterprise religion. The modern search for the spiritual, in fact, turns out to be, in very large measure, a rather selfish absorption by individuals in their own emotional well-being. The tradition of the Christian Church, on the other hand, conveyed a starkly different message. It was the message of Jesus. The world he knew, too, was full of spiritual disorientation and straining after religious inventiveness. He called it a faithless generation. Christ spoke of sacrifice, acceptance of the gravity of human sin and the need for repentance, of the realization by men and women that at the end of time there would be a fearful judgement, of a measure of denial of the world and its false priorities. These were not welcome words: the first was to be last, and the stone which the builders rejected was to become the cornerstone. Many were called and few were chosen. Religion, in this account of things, was not a therapeutic prop or a set of beautiful thoughts. It involved self-denial not emotional uplift – authentic religion is not even very nice since it goes against the grain of those (all of us) who are in a state of rebellion against God. The modern pursuit of the spiritual is ultimately a search for human happiness; the religion of Jesus, in contrast, is precisely about the sacrifices which we would not make if he did not command them. The 'spiritual' systems of today's private enterprise religion indicate our inability to accept that the world is a place of tribulation, and that its terms of reference do not cater for our every demand.

Forty Five

The darkening horizon

༄༅༆

The cruellest thing about old age is not consciousness of the immanence of death; it is the loss of personal independence in what is left of life. Some find that their lives are in practice taken over by the moral collectivism of the professional carers, or by the bureaucracy of the Social Services. Others, who experience the widespread scepticism about the truth of religion which is a feature of Western society, discover that the extension of life is apparently without any particular purpose: increased longevity is occurring in a culture which has little idea of what life itself is for. Most are lonely. The death of friends, the slipping away of the familiar as general shifts in society impinge upon individual perception, the loss of flexibility in those who begin to realize that their options are now expended, and the sense of being a burden to others, all result in fearful states of mind that often amount to despair. Then there is the impairment of mobility, accompanied by a degree of pain which, because so persistent, is sometimes unbearable. The true heroism of the old is unrecognized by the young, whose sense of the dreadful stages by which life is closed down is too remote to be real – and who in consequence regard the sufferings of the aged in an artificial perspective. Some of the old, too, undergo changes of personality, as illness destroys the familiar restraints, and a lifetime of kindness may turn into a catalogue of demands: this is especially harrowing for close relatives. So, as it happens, is the terrible lack of privacy in the public wards of hospitals. How appalling it is, both for the old and for their loved ones, to have to discuss the most intimate family affairs in the hearing of strangers. The modern culture of self-absorption and materialism does nothing to prepare us for the blighting effects of old age. We are unable to cope with what is actually a natural component of all life, and we regard the horrors of ageing as a kind of injustice.

A biblical view of the terms of human life is quite a corrective. There, in images that are sometimes no longer current but which can still confront us with the true nature of things, life is represented as unitary and transient. We are like the grass of the field, which withers and is no more. People are part of the created order, made out of the dust and returning to it. There is nothing which exempts us from the natural cycle of decay: God did not make a random and arbitrary world, but one whose processes and laws apply to us as to all other things. The teeming and seemingly incoherent mass of living stuff which adheres to the planet is indeed the material of which we are made; the other living things really are our brothers and sisters. If we prolong our lives by improving our diet, or changing our environment, or through medical capabilities, we must expect to prolong, also, the pains of old age. What we need to do is to recover some sense of the beauty of transience: it is actually the major feature of ageing, and it is the squalid disintegration of the body which is the minor. We are like passengers in transit to another country, facing the discomfort of travel. The disabilities of old age are a necessary preparation for the discarding of our earthly natures, a last terrible reminder of our frailty.

Forty Six

Triumph of the Ascension

৪০৫৪

There are quite a number of people who say they cannot believe in the existence of a God who appears to demonstrate such cruelty: living creatures prey upon one another; through genetic determination over which they have no control children are brought into the world with permanent disabilities; natural disasters destroy life on a massive scale; individuals are afflicted with horrific illnesses; many starve. But complaints about the order of things in fact reveal more about men and women and their demands and expectations than they do about the nature of God. We speak as if the world was fashioned just for us, and as if anything which causes us pain is somehow a violation of our entitlement to seamless happiness. God actually made the world and saw that it was perfect for his purpose. Not being gods ourselves we do not know what the purpose is – but we do know that at a late point in the creation God put us into the world. In the symbolic language of the Bible it is plain that humanity was established last: the people of the world, that is to say, were placed in a creation that was already perfect and it is we who have become alienated from perfection. The world was not set up to provide us with a painless existence, and it patently does not do so. But humanity was raised from the rest of the created things and given the capacities of reason and reflection. Our sense of pain is a consequence of our alienated condition, and our outrage that God did not exempt us from our material composition is simply unrealistic. We now know, due to advances of scholarly investigation, about the length of time during which something like recognizable humanity has inhabited the earth, and we now see that the preparation of mankind for the revelation of God's existence and laws has been a very extended one. Yet it is only in comparatively recent times that men and women have come to reject the concept of a divine being on the evidence of the existence of human suffering. What actually happened, of course, was that God sent his only Son into the world and he was crucified by us. It is human cruelty, not God's, which is the central event in human history.

Christ walked this earth and shared its sorrows. He was hungry in the wilderness, he wept over the death of a friend, he had pity for the sick, and he was saddened by the universal faithlessness. He was human as we are human, yet he was God in precisely the manner that we are not: sinless and perfect. In his earthly life he transcended the world, and in his Ascension, celebrated by the Church this last week, he completed his triumph over death. Men and women, too, are called to transcendence. But this is an age which does not want to transcend the world – it wants, on the contrary, to make it painless and materially accommodating. We always need to remind ourselves, however, that the world as it is is perfect for God's purpose, and that it is we who are out of joint, who make unreasonable demands of existence. The true followers of Christ are those who demand nothing. 'Not only so,' according to the Epistle to the Romans, 'but we also rejoice in our sufferings, because we know that suffering produces perseverance; perseverance character; and character, hope.'

Forty Seven

———————

The gift of the Spirit

ℰℐℭℬ

The Holy Spirit is the least recognized and least understood of
the persons of the Trinity. Is there really a mysterious force
which guides and directs the affairs of men and women, and
which is available to Christians? Men and women actually
observe forces and influences which mould and determine the
development of individual lives which, though perhaps complicated, are not at all mysterious. They see how good and bad
traits of character are produced by early conditioning and by
the random choices with which people are confronted, and that
some people of notable goodness have little or no indebtedness
to religious formation. They see how events produce outcomes
which require no special explanation, for they are the result of
the structures of society put in place by human design. They
see how sickness may sometimes be eradicated by the exercise
of determined will, through psychosomatic consciousness: no
divine interference is needed to plot the course of recovery.
They see how the propaganda of one age becomes the sacral
tradition of another – of how the historical and individual
embodiments of our values are put in place by men. Great
beneficial happenings, or beautiful personalities, which might
by some be seen as the fruits of spiritual growth, turn out to be
either chance products or purely earthly causes of false
adulation founded upon imperfect evidence. The lives of even
the greatest saints tend to be hedged about with very
conventional ambiguities. The Christianity of our day has
vibrant elements which emphasize the gifts of the Spirit – faith
healings, speaking in tongues, prophetic utterance, ecstatic

dance, and so forth. The history of the Church shows many such sequences. Are these really authentic evidences of the special presence of God; are they modern representations of the first visitations, described in scriptural images which must otherwise be regarded as symbolic, of the Paraclete?

Christianity is transmitted through a tradition of believers and not primarily through personal emotional experience. Since the collection of doctrines proclaimed by Christ are objectively true they exist independently of us or of our emotional condition. The religion of Jesus, that is to say, does not need any hidden or mysterious force for its survival in the world: it is passed on by the succession of the believers, of which the Church of our own day is the present representative. Now because Christian truth is committed to the agency of men it is conveyed in the images and symbols which men use, and much of the ephemera and cultural furnishings of each age and generation gets taken up in the process – only to be shed later as each group of believers sorts out afresh what is essential in Christ's message and what is merely contingent and accidental. Like all human undertakings this involves wrong judgements and ordinary mistakes. The gift of the Spirit preserves the people of God in all truth – in the essentials of what is really true. It is not a mysterious force but an extremely familiar presence: a Person, indeed, who determines the outcome of the Church's dialectic with the world. The Spirit is the garner of Providence, whose existence enables Christian people to be absolutely confident that they can transmit Christ to the next generation.

Forty Eight

In sickness and in health

ཐCབC

When men and women begin to lose their faith in God, or when they begin to 'prioritize' it differently, their highest and most deeply felt values descend from the heavens and become very much taken up with the world. It is no longer God who is venerated but man himself. In classic materialism the greatest priority becomes man and his needs, his welfare and his rights. These are characteristically then dressed up in great moral finery, and the sordid pursuit of personal security and well-being is represented in the language of ethical necessity; the highest good that can be imagined is to 'care' for others. In an extraordinary reversal of Christianity it is the love of neighbour – which actually comes after, and is dependent upon, the love of God – which becomes the sole canon in the secular law of humanity. In our society, at the present time, the sovereignty of man takes the form of preoccupation with health care.

There was a moment during the last British General Election when it seemed as if the outcome would be determined by the level of medical benefits available to an unfortunate girl with earache. Since then things have gathered pace. There are now few news bulletins which do not contain one or two items on hospitals, Health Service funding, the politics of health care, and the remuneration of health workers. Television screens are routinely filled with dramas and documentaries about hospitals and the emergency services; issues germane to this interest crop up in virtually every kind of discussion programme. Yet this is not really an indication of a public obsession with health but of an obsession with the politics of health – and of an equal obsession, which has a darker dimension, with individual entitlements. To the materialists, of course, this is all very wholesome, for here is evidence of a growing public disposition to moral consciousness: caring for others is obviously good. To what extent is the current health obsession really an indication of a caring society?

Jesus healed the sick because he had compassion on them. Each case of healing is actually recorded, however, not because of the cure as such but because of the claims to authority implicit in his actions. They were evidence of the Divine. Are there any claims behind the health priorities of the present day? It would seem not, and that the attempts to ethicize the preoccupation with health care are really rather hollow. There is a sour note in the public debate about the politics of health care, and a strong note of self-interest in the debate about benefits. They are, in fact, the present form which the age-old resort of men and women to accommodation with the world is taking. As in the explanation given by Christ of the Parable of the Sower: 'He also that received seed among the thorns is he that heareth the word; and the care of this world, and the deceitfulness of riches, choke the word, and he becometh unfruitful.' How like mankind to represent his material self-interest as a matter of high principle; how little authentic altruism resides within us. Real love of neighbour costs us dearly, but the present debate is about personal entitlements.

Forty Nine

Proclaiming the truth

∞⟡

The Holy Spirit guides Christian believers into all truth. Through all the successive changes of human culture, that is to say, the people of God can be certain that the Spirit will protect Christians in their task of preserving the purity and authenticity of Christ's message. They may get aspects of its application wrong: the teaching about, for example, human sexuality appropriate to one age may need to be modified in another; or the requirement to observe fasts suited to societies which are immediately dependent upon the cycle of the harvests may not necessarily assist the spiritual consciousness of the urban masses of the modern world. There is abundant opportunity for men and women to make errors of judgement as they operate upon information about the nature of the world that is forever changing. But the essential doctrines about God are guaranteed as immutable, and the Holy Spirit will keep the faithful – though they may be few – in knowing what they are. Exactly *how* few the faithful may be is a matter of considerable urgency in our day, since the desertion of orthodox Christian belief by the populations of the Western world seems set to continue. Modern life is no longer lived as if there were religious priorities, and those who do decide upon the need for religious faith tend to see that need in terms of an open-ended 'quest' whose outcome depends upon individual whim or choice rather than upon conscious assent to a known tradition of religious authority.

Knowledge of religion is transmitted through culture, and the key question therefore is how much is Christianity contributing to the formation of culture in Western societies today? How conscious are people of a Christian presence? Seemingly very little. We appear to be living on borrowed time, and the religious perceptions of men and women, to the extent that they persist, look like the declining after-glow of precepts and sentiments once derived from the family and the school but now only residually present there. Many of those who are worried about the lessening of religious commitment in our society are not really concerned with religious truth, furthermore, but with the positive utility of religion as an element of social and moral discipline. The practice of Christianity might, it is contended, counteract what is conventionally assumed to be the descent of society into crime. Yet the truly worrying thing for Christians ought to be the failure of the Church to penetrate the culture with a clear Christian message. Without that, the transmission of the faith, though not ultimately at threat, will be a minority affair indeed. People are very easily manipulated, and the history of the mass dictatorships and the foolish fashions of thought of the twentieth century suggest that the diffusion of education actually enhances, rather than diminishes, the extent to which they can be manipulated. It is no good for the Church to stand on one side and allow the ideological conflict to proceed without it. The Church has to be active in moulding the culture or it will not find a place in the resulting cultural terrain. It has to dirty its hands with the rough business of propaganda, just as Jesus did when he sent out the twelve to proclaim his word, and when he instructed his followers to go and teach all nations.

Fifty

Being born again

ಬಿಂ೦ಚಿ

St John the Baptist: the Church keeps this day in his honour. He is, in fact, less honoured than once he was by Christian people – not for any particular reason, but because of lost habit and the chilling spread of ignorance about their own faith among Christians themselves. The baptism of Christ, however, was the seminal event which immediately preceded his earthly ministry. To those who witnessed it something profoundly mysterious took place. The descent of God himself upon his Son. For John it was the occasion of the first recognition that Christ's ministry was to succeed his own. Jesus, he declared, was one greater than himself, the culmination of the prophetic tradition. In medieval iconography John is shown in his rough sheepskin clothes and with a lamb at his feet, a man acquainted with the austere calling of the wilderness, who set himself aside from the preoccupations of conventional society in order to proclaim the impending kingdom. Christ the King himself was, in his baptism, both giving himself to the religious forms of men and also transcending those forms through the unearthly presence of the dove of God. The whole purpose of his life with humanity was brought into the meaning of a single act: Jesus as truly man and truly God.

When Nicodemus, the ruler of the synagogue, subsequently came to Jesus by night to ask what he must do to become a member of that kingdom it was the language of baptism which Jesus used. You must be born again, he said, by water and the Spirit. It is that very radical consequence of baptism, whether made implicitly on behalf of a child by his sponsors, or by direct adult affirmation, which people in our world find so difficult. They don't want to be born again. They may well be hugely dissatisfied with things as they are, and are perhaps seeking a new meanings-system of thought, or maybe they are just looking for a release from the oppressive cares of the world. These, however, are conditions which reinforce the needs of the individual person; they derive from complaints about existing life, and generally from a sense that life owes them more than presently it seems to be delivering. What they do not want is to be told that their lives need to be restructured: to be born again, to start all over again. It is this utterly decisive break in life which people find so hard. They tend to see religious belief as a beautiful and reassuring addition to their lives, not as a set of obligations which turn them upside down. The life of the Spirit, Jesus told Nicodemus, is like the wind: you cannot control its direction, for that is the determination of God's creative power. People want certainty and security; the life of the Spirit, however, predicates earthly hazard – a new start, with everything therefore still to follow. So John the Baptist was the last of the old tradition and he dared to announce the new. The true follower of Christ is one who leaves the familiar behind and who reaches out to embrace the divine presence in the bleak human landscape; fortified by the promise of Christ to be present to the end of the world.

Fifty One

A lost generation

ॐଓଔ

People sometimes speak of the current interest in Western societies in New Age religion, or in the various cults and sects, as if they were an indication of a renewed vitality within religion itself. But it is not really so, and the long decline of institutional Christianity does not appear to have any compensation in a genuine expansion of interest in religion outside its boundaries. Those who are now involved in the new sects, or in constructing a religious system for themselves without reference to the historic Churches, would once have been adherents of the mainstream. The rise of the sects has been at the expense of traditional Christianity.

Now the decline of the institutional Church has not been primarily due to the spread and respectability of intellectual scepticism – as intellectuals, who after all write the books in which this notion is disseminated, claim. There is no straightforward link between, for example, the famous Huxley-Wilberforce debate about evolution and the declension of support for the Church. The emptying of the pews has been going on over a very long period, and is largely explicable in terms of lost habit. Most people do not desire to lose their faith, and they do not do so – at least, not initially. What they desire is more time and space to carry out life's obligations and pleasures. Jesus himself described the process in several of the parables. Men and women were called to be followers, but each in turn offers excuses: these are pressing obligations, some economic, some personal, which obtrude. The reasons they give are easily capable of moral interpretation, and would be instantly recognizable today. For they said, in effect, that duties relating to material welfare came first, for themselves and for the sakes of others. Jesus, it must be remembered, lived in an intensely religious culture, in an age which was preoccupied with religious issues; even so, he called the people of his time a faithless generation. What would he have made of ours?

The decline of the Church in modern Western society is largely produced, then, by lost habit. Homes are so comfortable, leisure activities are so concentrated in them due to the electronic revolution, the emphasis on family life increasingly disinclines members of a family to seek a life outside it. All forms of organized social activity, not just the Churches, are in decline. There is plenty of goodwill for Christianity, but its actual support is somehow left to others. In the press of life going to church has low priority. Parents retain a residual knowledge of the faith from their earliest days, but their children, who will never have had much instruction in Christian beliefs (and certainly not much in the space normally allocated to religious education in the schools), will have nothing to retain in their lives as the last embers of an extinguishing fire. Christianity is not being rejected in our society; it is being forgotten.

Fifty Two

The unreal world

❧

We seem unable to cope with life. No wonder the therapists are such a growing profession: people cannot cope with the ordinary misfortunes which are the natural lot of mankind and which, when encountered with realism and a balanced sense of our worth, are capable of inspiring us with nobility and altruism. People can no longer, for example, contemplate an accident without receiving counselling. Today when something goes wrong the immediate response is to try to locate blame – it is always the fault of somebody else or of government. The benchmark is a perfect world without misfortune; when something goes wrong it seems, to us, as if the world itself is to blame. We have also become addicted collectivists, and look to government and to public agencies as the means by which all human ills can be removed. The impulsion to seek compensation (reinforced, it is true, by the enterprise of solicitors seeking fees) is now the accepted accompaniment of an accident. As in the world of our distant ancestors, the worth of a human life is assessed for surviving relatives in cash terms. Behind it all lies an unrealistic view of human life itself and of the nature of the world in which that life is set.

It is easy to ridicule that element of traditional religious teaching which supposed that the lives of men and women in the world was full of woe, but that a heavenly compensation awaits beyond death – so that all kinds of injustices should be suffered here because better things are to come. There is a familiar modern caricature in which Christianity is seen as having been used in the past by the governing classes as a mechanism of social control. The caricature is actually more available than the evidence to support it, incidentally: the clergy of the past did not, as we like to think they did, usually behave with such insensitivity or stupidity. Their social terms of reference were different from ours, and the world has changed. The point, however, is that they did instruct their people realistically about the nature of life in the world. People were depicted as subject to misfortune; the world was not made in order to guarantee human repose; men and women behave badly towards one another; the rewards we expect we do not usually get; things go wrong. In the Christian view of the world people were raised by God from the rest of his creation – but they remain a material part of it, the very dust of which it is all made. But men and women today seek exemption from this status. They want the security of immortals, they expect an existence devoid of misfortune – a painless world of unbroken happiness. We see the pursuit of happiness, indeed, as the first goal of human life. It is not. But if we dedicate ourselves to perpetual happiness there will necessarily be a great gulf between our expectations and what the world actually delivers. The inclination of people today is to blame God for this; or to deny his existence because he has not created the world we would have created for ourselves. It is a very primitive view of things.

Fifty Three

———

Understanding the world

ೞರ

Despite appearances, and despite our experience of the way in which men and women manage to reduce everything to spiritual inconsequence, the world is actually an icon of eternity. All that we can know is expressed in earthly terms – our perception of reality itself, even our sense of the divine presence, is rendered in vocabulary and images which derive from our terrestrial context. To be known by us God became a man, and in him, Christians believe, the seen and the unseen worlds are joined. The earth as an icon of eternity represents two realms of experience: sceptics of religion will see the heavenly city as an invention by humanity, an unreal projection of its desire for significance, an ethereal artefact of its own devising; those who seek to be followers of religion will see the world as a material representation of the divine order, the heavenly city descended to the earth and habitable in time by those who can recognize its structures. Jesus spoke of the kingdom as a present reality – of eternal life as a condition entered now, with death as a moment of transition from the worldly icon to the spiritual truth of which it is a symbol.

Thus we, the men and women of the world, are called to become personal shrines of the truth, and to treat our lives not as utilities for the satisfaction of our desires but as spaces to be filled with the presence of holiness. It sounds such an unattainable ideal: how can we, as we actually are, self-seeking and flawed, be the shrines of ultimate truths? This is the great miracle of Christianity, that Jesus came not for the righteous but for sinners. His kingdom embraces the imperfect and the unclean, the criminals and the morally corrupt – all who, despite their earthly nature, call upon him to save their souls. And it is important that the conventionally virtuous always remember that. Jesus really did come for sinners, yet those who responded to him remained, still, burdened with their humanity, with their natures. God helps us to live better lives; but the reality about human life is, as St Paul said, that the good we would do we do not achieve. The Christian paradox, and the miracle of faith, is that men and women nevertheless become authentic reliquiae of true holiness even though the corruption and weakness of their natures does not change. Charity is the virtue whereby we accept the spiritual presence in others whilst being presented, simultaneously, with their earthly natures. Charity enables men and women to discern the heavenly city upon the human landscape, to see the materials of eternity among the rubble of human aspirations. Christ's celestial society includes the likes of us. It is that understanding of the world which gives true hope.

Fifty Four

_____

Whoever is perfect among you

ഇറ

The debate about crime in our society is continuing to reveal, and perhaps to foster, some very un-Christian views, and especially to point to a disagreeable desire for revenge both by the public and by the unfortunate victims of crime. But above all it is encouraging the categorization of criminals themselves as a particular species of humanity. They are demonized; they are considered people 'unlike us'. A very few may be: those who seem almost irredeemably vicious, or perhaps those like psychopaths, whose behaviour is dictated by mental orientation over which they have limited control. To apply the blanket description of 'criminal' to the large majority who fall foul of the law is extremely unhelpful, however. Very many of them, indeed, are precisely people 'like us', who because of weakness of character, or through the chance presentation of opportunity, or, sometimes, because of emotional necessity, commit crimes. Others are, in the broadest cultural perspective, the victims of society's moral conventions, guilty of offending against majority moral feelings which, though deeply held in one place or time, may be quite relative in their actual authority. Some sexual offences are of this genre and so are some crimes against property. The state, it is always necessary to remind ourselves, may clothe itself with the symbols of moral legitimacy, but is really just a majority who are using the coercive power of political authority to force everyone to obey their moral inclinations. The degree to which those inclinations

_107_

have authenticity is made to depend on the level of acceptance they can command. What is the moral authority, for example, that the state can appeal to when it decides to censor a particular film – when a majority, through its agencies, decides what others can see? What is the code it is enforcing? Is it the Christian moral law – in what many now claim is a secular society? Does the enforced morality depend on its inherent truth or because it attracts majority support? If the latter, does anyone really believe that moral truth can be determined by the counting of heads? Or is there a 'Natural Law' which supplies the moral content in all places, as true in the most primitive societies as in the most advanced? Modern cultural relativism has begun to obliterate the distinction between primitive and advanced cultures, so the issue is complicated still more. A lot of behaviour natural to mankind is atrocious, and morality becomes an affair of artificial constraints – who should decide what to select? The worst things that people routinely do are not within law anyway: the daily acts of personal insensitivity and greed. Christians should be clear that they are responsible for extending the forgiveness that Christ holds out to anyone who regrets their shortcomings, and that the largest part of the 'criminal' population consists of people just like themselves.

Fifty Five

The earthly snare

೮つೞ

It used to be the aim of the now disbanded and discredited Communist regimes to persuade their people that humanity was the measure of all things, that there were no transcendent realities, and that it was man and his material condition which was the sovereign consideration of life on earth. Because people also had emotions and responded to cultural stimuli the human 'spirit' was catered for by the provision of approved art, literature, music, and so forth; the 'spiritual' dimension of life was expressed in wholly secular terms to convey the sense of humanity at the highest – but still material – consciousness. Children in the schools, particularly, were subjected to rigorous programmes of indoctrination, which included the explicit denigration of religion – which was represented as a mere human phenomenon, either expressing the class interests of a given level of society, or as a means of social control. Of course, humanity being the way it is, the policy was not always successful, and when the various regimes disintegrated all manner of unapproved views about human life were found to have survived within the sub-cultures. The materialist understanding of mankind had, on the other hand, meanwhile taken root among the intelligentsia of the non-Communist world, and is now thriving as never before – education, again, providing a primary means of indoctrination. It has a benign countenance, however, and is not recognized for what it is. In the Western countries the 'spiritual' dimension of human life has been, as in the former Marxist states, secularized, but in an incoherent fashion, without an ideological label.

The beginning and end of our troubles is that we think too highly of ourselves, as materialists always do. Now that mankind and his material needs have come to be regarded as the highest good, we judge the world in relation to what it offers us, to the extent that it satisfies our craving for material welfare and security. Even religion is assessed – and even by the religious themselves – according to its capability to satisfy our emotional needs, our craving for a meanings-system. Moral values, too, are determined by immediate human requirements: the worst we can imagine is racism, the best we can imagine is caring for others. It is all about human welfare. There is a conventional assumption that religion itself should be centred in human rights and social justice – thus, as in the past, investing our social and cultural preoccupations with sacred significance. Humanity has become divine, and we find ourselves believing only in a God who is dedicated to thinking as highly of us as we think of ourselves. But men and women are actually enveloped in sin, and God is a judge as well as a being of infinite love. The parables of Jesus point to a discriminating sovereign, who demands that we repent, and, in effect, use our lives not in the pursuit of personal welfare but in the exploration of realities outside of humanity and its supposedly pressing needs.

Fifty Six

Something to be thankful for

୫**ଓ**୯ଓ

It is possible that our successors will look back upon the condition of life in the twentieth century as a kind of golden age. For there are so many benefits available to us. There is a general acceptance that each person is entitled to the public provision of a wide range of services and decencies. It is a time when medical advance has radically diminished infant mortality, and when new drugs are capable of containing many diseases – a condition which is plainly not going to go on for much longer. Natural resources are still able to provide cheap energy, and we are using them up, indeed, in the probably false assumption that future generations will discover new means of generating power for themselves. The public provision of welfare, which we have come to take for granted, also has a limited future since in both the public and the private provision of benefits, the members of those earning the wealth to operate the system is diminishing, just as the population is developing longevity: right now is the most favourable time to be in receipt of a pension, in view of the bleak future ahead. Despite our impression that the world is permanently given over to conflict, and despite the human cull produced by two global wars, the twentieth century has in reality seen a large measure of repose from strife for many people: so much so, in fact, that in the developing world the population is growing out of proportion to its resources. There has not been a nuclear catastrophe, and we are still, just, living at a time before nuclear weapons pass into the hands of bandit states and actual individual bandits. There is, above all, greater personal liberty than there has ever been in the history of humanity. People in Western societies may choose their own religion and lifestyle; they can select their own marriage partner and live where they like; they can shop around to pick out their own cultural preferences; the leisure revolution, and the availability of television and personal retrieval systems, widens horizons in a manner quite beyond the expectations of our predecessors. Compared with the moral totalitarianism that probably awaits us in the future, the present is a kind of untypical interlude in the development of humanity, when people have a more significant control over their own lives than they are ever likely to have again.

How do we respond to all these benefits? It is with constant complaints, and an uninformed belief that human life today is somehow uniquely disagreeable. In its most favourable light it may be said that this demonstrates a sort of divine discontent – that we always have the capacity of imagining a flawless universe. In reality, however, it is another indication of the feckless ingratitude of a people who are increasingly unmindful of the goodness of the God who gave us life at all.

Fifty Seven

On leaving the world
ഋ‍ഇ

As people grow older they often achieve a remarkable clarity of vision. Its chief characteristic is a reorientated sense of priorities, so that the things which had been first in their lives become last, and the last first. They find that the material possessions and the security – including the emotional security – which had so preoccupied them for a lifetime, gradually seem less valuable or essential. Sometimes, it is true, this reordering of things is summarily induced by a shocking change of circumstance. Personal immobility is often the cause: this necessitates leaving a beloved home, or the immediate company of loved people, and everything familiar that seemed to have defined what they are is lost for whatever remains of existence in the world. There is no deprivation so cruel as the exchange of a home for the relatively impersonal environment of the hospital ward or the room in a residential hostel. The consolations of relatives and friends, or the supererogatory concern of the professional carers, is no substitute for the material associations in which the familiar circumstances of an independent life are unfolded. The wise will of course recognize that they are what they are, and not what they possess; but that is not really a very adequate consolation when all that is familiar is suddenly taken away.

There may be, then, no effective palliation for the inevitable upheavals attendant upon ageing – humanly speaking. But the experience can nevertheless be turned to productive purpose. For it at least is a reminder that the world is not the end and destiny of men and women, and that our time here is not intended to be used up in the pursuit of comfort and security. Jesus always indicated that his kingdom began in the world, for here are the only building materials of the heavenly city that we can understand and use: but he insisted that the kingdom was not worldly – that the materials were to be fashioned in order to withstand death, and death's disagreeable preliminaries. The house of our lives must be built upon a rock; we are to be dwelling places of the Holy Spirit. Everything that defines what we are, in short, must be a quality of our interior lives and not of our material circumstances. We are like people on a lengthy journey, who must take all that is necessary for the voyage along with us. Jesus himself owned nothing: he had no house, and did not have a family of his own. He sought out the desert places to be alone with his Father, and it was the barren landscapes which he converted into the riches of the kingdom. Its citizens were the poor and the ritually unclean – barren people in the judgement of society, who yet became the princes of the eternal country to which all are travelling.

Fifty Eight

Enduring truths

৪০৫জ

How poorly equipped people today are to cope with the kinds of personal misfortune which once were recognized as the normal lot of men and women! Our first inclination when something goes wrong is to find someone else to blame, and then to seek compensation – as if real life is an uninterrupted sequence of predictable and benign events whose interruption is a gross injustice. We are, in effect, victims of our own expectations. We posit total security as the term upon which life is to be lived by us and our families, and are then outraged when fate throws something else across our path. If that dislocation of our self-proclaimed serenity is something inseparable from the nature of self-proclaimed things – the consequence of a natural disaster or a fatal or debilitating illness – then we give up belief in the divine source of life, for we cannot believe in a God who is not dedicated to guaranteeing our happiness. And if the interruption to our expectations is produced by social effects – crime for example – we rush to legislate it out of existence, or, if that should seem unavailable as a species of redress, we seek legal compensation. The more we expect complete security, the less real security do we achieve, since we are forever extending the boundaries of the secure to include more and more aspects of daily existence. No wonder the modern world impresses so many people today as being more hazardous than the world of our predecessors! In some areas, of course, the scale of risks *has* increased: nuclear warfare may kill people on a larger scale than was envisaged in past conflicts, but there are far more people than in the past, and the balance of things remains about the same. What has changed is our ability to cope with the imperfections which are in a steady state in all life.

This also describes the depth of our materialism in modern society. Human need, human security, and the sovereignty of the human pursuit of happiness, have become the overriding entitlements of life on earth. Even when we speak of 'spiritual' values, it is frequently in the secularized sense of personal 'enrichment': spiritual values are perceived as things like music and art and literature – things which are thought to add to the fullness of the human personality. Actually they go well with the goal of personal security, for a human person so invested with all this culture is a valuable asset. But authentic spirituality is acquainted with transcendence. It resides in the emptying out of our expectations, our embracing of the hazardous – since it is located in transience, and its effects are glimpsed when the familiar and the secure are denied, and the world grows cold. That is precisely why modern people do not want to know about it. Take away their addiction to themselves and there is nothing left.

Fifty Nine

Relative judgements

୫ටඋଓ

In many ways the health and vitality of an institution may be judged by the degree of respect it shows for its own history and traditions. Those outside the institution are likely to take their cue, in assessing it, from its own self-evaluation. One of the troubles for Christianity today comes precisely from its own evident loss of confidence in its own past. Christians, indeed, almost seem to take delight in confessing the deficiencies in their own record, especially in relation to the kinds of issues involving human rights and social justice which now form the moral consciousness of modern secular humanism. A continuous tradition of two millennia of caring for the sick, tending the young, providing shelter for outcasts; of administering charity, and providing the dignity of spiritual citizenship for those whom the world despised, has been ignored – or perhaps is no longer known about. Christians seem to be among the first to represent their own past as a heap of social injustices, in which the Church was found to have supported every kind of wrong action, from the slave trade to sex inequality. They see the past, too, as a catalogue of prejudice and intolerance: theirs is a Church which persecuted those with different opinions.

Now the history of Christianity, like the record of any institution or tradition of ideas, shows that it was always and unavoidably penetrated by the cultures through which it passed. The past is unlike the present: it had different priorities and preoccupations, and layer upon layer of these got added to the Christian tradition – and have accordingly been dug out and discarded from time to time. The religion of Christ is a progressive revelation; it develops over time. It is also historical: it works through the material and the actual; its content is defined in relation to the knowable and concrete universe of our experience. Its adherents are merely human, and whilst Christ himself through the Holy Spirit guarantees their faithfulness in the essential truths about the divine nature, when it comes to applications in the world, the moral frailty and blinkered vision of men and women inevitably obtrudes. Few in the West today would care to ransack the social record of Islam or Hinduism in the way the record of Christianity is treated, for they would not wish to incur the charge of insensitivity to the religious convictions of their adherents. Yet Christianity is ceaselessly attacked, in the classroom and in the television documentary, for its past record in relation to such issues as slavery. Who attacks Islam, whose adherents invented the slave trade? The tolerance between the religious traditions of the world rests on something more measured than this unequal treatment. The love of God extends to all his children, in all religious traditions – it is we who are unmindful of it.

Sixty

Called by love

༄ C༄

At the centre of Christianity is the person of Jesus: God, not as a distant mysterious force, the awesome first mover of the universe, but God as a person who may be known and addressed directly. He is the consolation of the lonely and the hope of the dispirited. It was Jesus who welcomed 'those who travail and are heavy laden', and whose kingdom is not reserved for the good or the pure but for everyone who regrets their failings and seeks his forgiveness. To those horrifyingly impressed by the dreadful bleakness of life – which should be all of us, from time to time – Jesus extends himself: not as some explanation of the meaning of things, and he does not remove the pain. The Ascension of the Lord lifts humanity with Christ; the earth itself, irradiated by the divine presence in its very creation, is joined in the triumph of the Saviour to a realm of existence which in every sense passes our understanding. Yet there, at the very congress of the seen and the unseen worlds, is the personal friend of sinners, whose supreme concern for his people bypasses the preoccupations which make us frightened. In Jesus is life, a sacred gift which we should be ashamed of regarding, as we sometimes do, as a burden: we are in the presence of the crucified Lord who took our burdens upon himself.

We are in the world only for the time being, and the world defines the limitations of our vision. Thus we actually see Jesus through his body which is still in the world – the Church. For the message of Christ was delivered to a living and immortal tradition, and it is interpreted by those who stand in the midst of it. This is the pivot of the divine paradox: perfect truth was entrusted to sinners. But it is no paradox in the end, since the fallen are raised up, and although that does not take away their weakness and wickedness, it does make them capable of bearing the forgiveness of Christ to others. And that is the office of the Church through the ages. It is important, for that vocation, that the Church is composed of people of all sorts. It is a sample of the world, a cross-section of the tree of life. Here are the virtuous and the corrupted, and here are the intelligent and the dull, the gifted and the mundane, the strong and the weak. The Church is open to the criminal and the conventional, to people of variant sexualities, to advocates of hugely differing schemes for the social and the political order. Defined by the gift of forgiveness, and the accessibility of the person of Jesus, the Church is universal. Yet so many who would seek its embrace are actually put off by its very human composition. They see that church members are, humanly speaking, capable of all kinds of nastiness. What should they expect? A society of the forgiven is a reflection of the real world. In contrast to the imperfections of men and women, the mercy of Jesus is without blemish.

Sixty One

Master and friend

ॐ

The disclosure of God, Christians believe, was very precise. It took place within a particular society at a time chosen so that a conjunction of cultures would give Christianity an immediate universality. Jesus was rooted in the Jewish interpretation of God and yet spread his truth over the entire religious landscape of the ancient world. Thus Christianity was Judaic in theology, Hellenistic in the definition it received at the early Councils, Roman in its organization, and Egyptian in a number of its popular teachings which had affinity with resurrection cults. Yet it was also very precise: the universal truth of God was expressed within an exact tradition. Jesus did not tell the people that they could sense the divine in all kinds of ways – as we tend to expect the divine presence to be in the modern world – and that they could select the one most appropriate to their personal needs. He told them, on the contrary, that the gate was narrow and that the entry to his kingdom required very definite beliefs. Whoever would follow him, furthermore, had to make decisive changes in his life: he was to leave family and friends for his sake, to take up the cross, to be born again.

Now these are all characteristics quite at variance with our modern understanding of religion. People today do not feel attracted to the fact that Jesus was located at a precise place in historical development. What they see is not a universal truth given a singular expression, but a person confined within the circumstances of his day; what they want is a generalized God, a kind of personal summary of all the higher and beautiful thoughts that people have about one another in the world.

_121_

Modern people, that is to say, are hostile to the idea of dogma – of rendering universal truths in precise categories. The very word has become pejorative. So they regard all religious ideas as more or less equal, and select from among them according to personal inclination: what does something for them. This is religion as therapy; it elevates human need above the objective commands of the Divine, and the result is the religion of humanity. Those religious ideas are approved which express and sanctify the preoccupation with human welfare. Existing religious traditions, like Christianity, are reinterpreted (often by their own adherents) as being essentially dedicated to the cosmic vision of the professional carers. Religion, in the process, is relativized, its purposes subordinated to human need. The God of such a religious understanding becomes unreal, for a divinity defined in terms of material welfare will be found wanting. He is not delivering the required results: people *do* get fearful diseases, *are* extinguished in disasters, suffer pain, and lead apparently pointless lives. The Christian God, however, suffered along with humanity in the agony of crucifixion. He calls us not to material security, but to repentance.

Sixty Two

Divine essentials

❧❦

A lot of people are very unclear as to exactly why they believe in Christianity. For some it is a general disposition of life, something learned in childhood in the home and the school, and which remains gently present as a kind of personal reference, rarely questioned, and very rarely activated either. For others religious faith has been acquired through enquiry. But why was the enquiry set on foot? There are not many who pursue truth for its own sake, whose involvement with religion derives from a disinterested excursion into philosophical alternatives. It is perhaps safe to take it that many whose faith depends upon active choice expect to get something out of it. It was always so. Religion in traditional society was a means of social identity, an authenticator of the prevalent moral code, a way of attaining a relationship with the past record of the social unit, and a means of getting daily help from the encompassing presence of the ancestors or the saints. In the post-Romantic world in which we now live, people also look to religion as a source of beautiful reflection, and a way (now reinforced by ecological obsessions) of reconciling nature and human understanding. For people in modern Western society religion is also regarded as a means of emotional enrichment, as an area where loving relationships receive a hallowed expression, and as a dimension to life which imparts meaning and purpose.

None of these considerations are actually very helpful in understanding what God really wills for us. The fact is that religion is something we don't particularly want to know about. It is about obedience to commands which often run contrary to our own inclinations, about our recognition of the sinfulness of our own natures. Religion is progressive: the Bible describes a people who gradually discover the will of God over a long period, and this progression was meant to carry on. Christ was not the terminator of human history, but the one who brought salvation. The revelation made of God in him was perfect and all-sufficient, but it was not intended to be static. The world as God has made it is in a permanent state of change, and as men and women join with him in using the mechanics of the creation so their appreciation of the progressive nature of the divine revelation should be enhanced and advanced. Elements of primitive religious understanding then need to be abandoned – including some quite modern ones, like the pervasive notion that religion itself is all about human emotional satisfaction. The more we understand our material context, the more we should appreciate our essential wretchedness. It is human sin which is written large on the pages of the human story, and we should never forget it. The greatness and the love of God, is that he extends forgiveness.

Sixty Three

The last are first

ജ

The sense that inessential things are falling away is one of the gifts of old age. All kinds of preoccupations and urgencies carried around in a lifetime of worries somehow no longer seem so pressing, and ambitions which once were so desirable may seem, with the benefit of hindsight, to have been quite wrongly inspired. A wise person will recognize that they are better off for *not* having achieved some of the objectives they had once set themselves – since the accumulation of experience, changed circumstance, and the passing of time itself have altered their own priorities. Many of the things we have managed to achieve eventually turn out to be dust and ashes anyway; they did not deliver the benefits anticipated. Old age is a time for reflection. But it is also the occasion for something more. In the parable of the labourers in the vineyard, Jesus taught that those who came last into employment were equal to those who were first: that the mercy of God is without limitation and that it is never too late to receive it. The wise will convert the rather unwelcome experience of ageing to good account if, like the last of the labourers, they are active in seeking new insights into God's will for their lives. When the main work is over there is time – time to reflect, in a quantity unknown since childhood. And as life grows longer due to improvements in nutrition, medication, and shelter, the occasions for enrichment of personal understanding are increased. The sadness of the modern world is that so few recognize old age as a time to be used for spiritual productivity, and the extra years slip away without evident result. It was one of the virtues of the ancient world that society saw the wisdom residing in the old – who had seen the problems of the world before. But those who use their time improvidently are foolish: and there is, as they say, no fool like an old fool. Knowledge, in our world, is forever changing and expanding, but wisdom is constant, the same amount around today as there has always been. Wisdom, however, requires cultivation, and the wisdom of the old is only of value, to themselves and to others, when old age itself is made the realm of active discovery.

Humanity thinks too highly of itself, and makes unwarranted claims to repose and understanding which the world as it is cannot satisfy. As a species we are not really worth bothering about. But the goodness of God, who made us for purposes we do not comprehend, guides the lives of even the most lonely and unloved of his children, and dignifies each with the gift of his love. For the aged, in particular, there is a special opportunity to prepare the spiritual garden in which the flowers of spirituality may grow and flourish. God calls us out of the world as he wills, and no one knows the time or the place of that calling. The one certainty is that we only hear his voice if we have first learned the vocabulary of grace during our lives.

Sixty Four

The world as it is

෨෬

The Gospel records that when Jesus saw a man who had been blind from his birth, the disciples asked him 'who did sin, this man or his parents, that he was born blind?' (John 9:2). It is just the kind of question we are liable to ask today. 'Why did God allow this to happen?' people say when they note some fearful occurrence or some apparent cruelty of the creation. Or, 'what did I do to deserve this?' The truth is that the universe was not made for us, and it is not the one, given our own priorities, that we might have chosen. God made the world and then placed us in it. The creation is perfect for his purpose – which we do not know, and will not, while we are in the world and inseparable from the things here which condition us. Left to ourselves we would probably order for the universe, as we might order from a restaurant menu, all the things which we imagine will furnish a painless and happy existence, for ourselves and for those whom we love. Humans being as they are we might well, of course, order rather less pleasing circumstances for those who irritate us: but then in our ideal world, presumably, there would be no irritation. There would also be virtually no meaning. A plateau of everlasting contentment suggests no creativity, no inventiveness, no joining with the divine scheme in exploring and developing the planet – all of which things derive from human discontent, itself inspired by our capacity to conceive of better things. Life is clearly not a cruel trick of random chance, as sometimes it seems: it is intended to be the opportunity of discovery, and it is through pain as much as through delight in the terrain of our pilgrimage that value is added to existence and people grow in understanding. This is not necessarily, probably not usually, an intellectual experience. People of all sorts and all capacities are placed in the world, and it is the message of Jesus that all of us shall have to be again like little children to enter his kingdom. We have, that is to say, to surrender ourselves trustingly to God's will; and his will is expressed in the only world we can know about. The real world, the world as it is, discloses the intentions of God for us, and to be wise is to make our hopes and our expectations coincide with things seen. To strive to make life more redolent of the qualities of the divine love, to use our arts and our science to join in the divine plan, is the perfect expression of our humanity. It is what we are made to do. Our lowest expression is to make our own material welfare sovereign, and then to complain about a world in which it is not attained. The reply of Jesus to the question of the disciples about the blind man says it all: neither the man nor his parents had sinned, and his dreadful affliction was 'that the works of God should be made manifest in him'. The immediate sign of that was a demonstration of the healing power of Jesus. The permanent sign of it is our use of the powers God gives us to make the earth a place of discovery and meaning.

Sixty Five

———

There abide until you depart

൦൪

If Christians today are asked to say what is the first and most important duty of their faith, their priority is likely to be ethical in nature. They will say it is to be caring, or to promote justice, or perhaps even to seek the happiness of others. The heroes of the faith are the agents of human welfare. If we would know the priority set by Jesus, however, we shall find it in the declaration that the first and greatest commandment is to love God, and that the second is the love of neighbour. Jesus did not just wander the countryside teaching his truths as if they were self-evidently going to be recognized and adopted: he founded a Church – a body of people who were to succeed his body on earth when the time came for him to return to the Father. The Church began when (as we read in the sixth chapter of St Mark's Gospel) he trained teachers to go into the towns and villages to proclaim his message. They were sent out in pairs, instructed to take nothing for their journey, and to be dependent upon those to whom they were sent. 'And they went out,' we read, 'and preached that men should repent.' There, then, at the very beginning, was this divine priority. The first message of Christ to his Church was the need for repentance. It was not an exhortation to moral elevation or to welfare – that came second. The missioners sent out were also told to anoint the sick and so to fulfil the second commandment, the love of neighbour. But first came an admission of sin, the essential preliminary to the reception of salvation. It is that which we neglect today. The largest part of the ministry of Jesus was taken up with exactly the same call for men and women to recognize their sin. The days were evil, and the days of men were numbered. Eternity presses near to us, and what is wrong with each one of us is infinitely greater than our own capacity for self-correction. Humanity is out of joint at the very axis of its being; our most dedicated attempts at serving others, even, are flawed by the ambiguous motivation that is germane to the nature and context of men. So without the priority of repentance, any attempt to achieve love of neighbour will be fatally flawed too – a mere expression of benevolent intention, a psychological impulsion, an extension of self-interest, or perhaps a desire to win the admiration of others. Jesus spoke time and time again about judgement. Our lives in the world end in judgement, and the need to admit and confess our sinfulness is the means by which each person receives the grace which alone creates our openness to the mercy of God. In our own strength and action we can never cancel out the enormous debit of our sin: forgiveness is a free gift of God, but to receive it we have to recognize the existence of our inherent corruption. This is the ancient message of Christianity, the truth first conveyed by those taught to be his messengers by Christ himself. The splendour of eternity is so close to each one of us; we need only to see that we have first to reach out to the author of forgiveness.

Sixty Six

Living love

ඞඔ

Many people find it difficult to believe in a God who has
created a world like our world. They behold a pitiless creation, a
mass of living things whose existence depends upon mutual
destruction. The more science reveals about the nature of life,
the more it becomes clear that in order to receive nourishment
and to survive, each creature, including ourselves, must absorb
or kill others. The immune system of our own bodies destroys
countless thousands of living entities each day – tiny cells – in
order to preserve us from illness or malfunction. Before our
knowledge became so exact, life could more easily be identified
as possessed of meaning: now it seems merely a phenomenon.
Our lot has only seemed tolerable because we discriminate
about the *size* of the living things we destroy in order to live.
From the youngest age children are given toys which are
replicas of furry animals – creatures they can endow with
human characteristics and find appealing. The bacteria in their
own bodies, however, are no less living things: seen in
magnification they are often of astonishing beauty. It is just
that they are less readily credited with sympathetic qualities
than furry animals. It is, after all, replicas of bears or of rabbits
which are handed to infants in prams, not fluffy versions of
tuberculosis bacteria. We disguise the bleak reality of the
nature of life on earth by dividing living things into those of
which we can have immediate knowledge from those which are
invisible, and by allowing ourselves emotional illusions about
the extent to which appealing animals may be considered
substitute humans. The notion that there can be a God who has

---

131

actually set up a world which exists by an everlasting process of mutual preying is, for many, too shocking to be a possibility. The more people become aware of the nature of life, through the dissemination of knowledge, the more we can expect an increase of intellectual scepticism. God will be rejected on moral grounds; his creation lacks the ethical relationships between living things that we ourselves consider essential. Yet the biblical view of the creation always saw it as an arena of mutual dependence. The whole creation is described as existing not for our purposes – for humanity was placed in the creation last – but for God's. Such meaning as may be attached to it by us derives from our co-operation with the divine scheme: meaning is, humanly speaking, imposed on reality by our discoveries. This is assisted, Christians believe, by the fact that God has also 'revealed' aspects of his own nature by entering the understanding of humans through his own historical presence – first in the religious traditions of ancient peoples, and then in the person of Christ. What men and women discovered, through extended relationship with the world, was the very meaning, in the form of moral sense and observable order, which we now take so much for granted. We also discover the mercy of God. For he lifts humanity out of the buzzing mass of living things, and endows us with the capacity to reason and to reflect, and to find purpose.

Sixty Seven

All Souls

ଛଠ

The modern interest in the occult and the supernatural is puzzling. As the daily references of life become increasingly secular, people seek some kind of substitute for formal religion in a preoccupation with the macabre and the fantastic. It is even presented as entertainment: seen in the television programmes in which people recount their own supposed experiences of supernatural visitations, and in the popularity of both juvenile and adult comic books in which adventure is set amidst counter-worlds of horrific and nightmarish surrealism. There is no way of quantifying the enormous numbers of people who believe in the possibility of some sort of contact with the dead, and every Christian minister will know from episodes of his or her own ministry how many equate some allegedly supernatural event with evidence of religious experience. We are living in an age of faith indeed; the advance of human society into materialism is being unexpectedly accompanied by a resurgence of popular superstition.

The Church has always warned against involvement with the occult, and it was not just because here was seen to be a dangerous realm where the souls of men and women could be captured by evil. When personal demons were part of popular culture, and when darkness ushered the spirits of hell into the habitations of men, it was natural enough that the Church of light should discourage the means by which evil could be focused. But the knowledge which the Church has also always fostered, through its promotion of education down the centuries, has surely dispelled a world-picture in which actual demons can take possession of souls. The recent revival of Hallowe'en, presumably aimed at children and inspired by commercial considerations, is doubtless harmless enough, since few are likely to recognize its distant ideological affinities. But when it comes to contact with the dead – given a renewed popularity by the Victorian penchant for spiritualism – there is a serious threat to Christian understanding. For the Church did not condemn attempts to raise the spirits of the dead because it sensed a rival in the area of spiritual power, but because spiritualism obscured the real and authentic accessibility of the unseen world. Serene and mysterious, everywhere present and forever beckoning to eternity, the society of the departed is part of the Christian view of the world. As the Lord descends to the altar in the celebration of the Eucharist, Christians believe, the greater part – the far greater part – of those present in the Church are the unseen ranks of the blessed. Angels also gather at the table of the Lord, and it is the living who are the witnesses to an eternal act of which they are a part. So transience is converted into the permanence of the celestial presence, and the seen and the unseen worlds intermingle. Men and women do not need the silly paraphernalia of the paranormal to be in a relationship with the dead: the Christian life, properly understood, is the everlasting company of those who love God.

Sixty Eight

Intercession

❧❧

People have always needed to lay their most deeply felt concerns before their gods, and in primitive understandings of religion it was thought necessary for the gods to be appeased as well. Hence the sacrificial altars and the votive offerings which characterized the religions of antiquity – and some surviving ones. The walls of pagan shrines were covered with incised petitions, as may be seen to this day in the lower terraces at Delphi. The Christian religion incorporated aspects of all this as well, and the Church has always encouraged its members to place their needs and anxieties before the throne of grace. Within Orthodoxy and Catholicism the custom of votive offerings persisted in symbolic form, and tokens of thanksgiving for answered prayers still movingly adorn their great healing sanctuaries. This is, in some particulars, all very salutary. But there is a need for prayer to be educated. God does not grant what we ask but what he wills for us. He has made a world which operates according to the laws he has established: the material universe has both ordered and random dimensions, and the sum total of its unimaginable complexity is known only to God. He does not work by magical means but through creation, and we are a part of it. We are determined in our knowledge and physical fate by its laws of operation. If we would be realistic in our prayers we should ask not for some miraculous suspension of those laws, which would run counter to normal experience, but for acceptance of what the Lord ordains. Humanly speaking, of course, we shall always be inclined to lay the needs and health of our loved ones, and of ourselves, before God: it is one of the characteristics of the sensitivity which describes our difference from the inarticulate and non-moral part of the creation. Our prayers should not, however, be a checklist of welfare demands, a trouble-free scenario for living. They should be in the grain of reality. We should not ask for full understanding of God's will, for we do not have the capacity for that; some things are reserved for the understanding of those members of Christ's body who exist in eternity. We should pray by first identifying our subject – 'Lord I pray *about* . . .' or 'Lord I bring before you my worry concerning . . .'. Then a moment of reflection in which our needs and anxieties may be rehearsed before God. And then, as the main part of the prayer, a call for God to help us to accept his will in the particular matter of our concern. God's purpose, and not ours, is going to be done anyway, and there is no reason why it should coincide with what we regard as our own best interest. The most fearful pains and deprivations may help us and those whom we love: it is not for us to assume a knowledge of the outcome of our lives. The purpose of life is not the perpetual satisfaction of our desires, but a progressive growth in spiritual formation, as we fashion that part of ourselves which is to endure everlastingly. Prayer is an occasion to love the author of all created things, and to trust him to guide our lives into greater light. His will, not ours, be done.

Sixty Nine

The rule of life

ಬಂಛ

Discussion of medical ethics and allied issues seems to be switching from the area of moral authority to the area of personal rights. In the abortion debate, for example, more is now heard about 'a woman's right to choose' than about the application of moral law concerning the treatment of life. In questions like the limits of medical technology in deciding what constitutes death, or the degree of intervention permissible in gene therapy manipulation of the human person, there are plainly matters which would once have been immediately recognized as belonging to moral law. Now they are often discussed in relation to human convenience or clinical efficiency. It says a great deal about the slide of society into materialism. None of these issues are easy, and few are one-dimensional; there is right and wrong mixed together in a single problem, and many grey areas, some of which yet require further advances of knowledge for decisive consideration. For Christians, however, the world may treat the human person as it will but for them there are some enduring moral guidelines, applicable whether the issue in question is simple or complicated. First of these is the sovereign principle that our lives are not our own to dispose of as we will. Humans, like the rest of the creation, belong to God: he entrusts us with a life which remains his, and which returns to him for judgement at the end of time. Nothing should be done by us to that life – or to a potential life – which is inspired by mere convenience. There should be, for Christians, no 'social' grounds (to employ the current euphemism) for determining the fate of life: only moral grounds applied to the fate of what is not a piece of tissue, but part of a spiritual being. 'Social', in this context, actually relates to another concept, 'the quality of life'. But our idea, which is relative to place and culture, as to what constitutes 'quality' living should never override the gift of God. For God did not introduce the human person to the world in order that his or her existence should be unencumbered by responsibilities, or free of poverty or whatever may be thought to impair the chances of security. Threat to life is another matter. God made men and women with the capacities of reason and understanding, and the use of science to join God in the creative development of human existence – to alleviate bodily disorders, or to avoid unnecessary death – is clearly different from the use of knowledge to satisfy mere personal convenience. Life is not sacred, and there is nothing sacred about us. It is God who is sacred. It is not our sanctity that needs to be accorded priority, therefore, but God's. Our bodies are the vehicles of our spirit: both, it must be remembered, are God's. We have no 'rights' in relation to him, only the duty to determine what he wills and to try to act in accordance with it. His law transcends our convenience.

Seventy

Now and ever shall be

ঔ৻ঙ৺

It may be that it is the wise who are lonely, and the foolish who bluster through life too preoccupied with themselves and their busy social instincts to recognize the bleak truths of reality. For God sends us into this world of suffering on our own, made to have a relationship with him forever, but for a season to be cut off from our true home, strangers in a foreign land. Sometimes loneliness is an experience which grows with age, as the loved ones and companions who have shielded us from the stark nature of our real situation begin to be called away. Sometimes loneliness is recognized from an early age as an unavoidable condition of our natures, as one of the characteristics of personality that gives us identity. Many are actually extremely lonely though they are successfully married, or in some other close relationship which, so it should seem, might have prevented their affliction. Loneliness is a condition of mind, not a social consequence. It is the sense that we are horrifyingly separated from the things which seem to us to afford consolation and meaning to others; it is the sensation of singularity – that we are responsive to no external source for interior cultivation. Loneliness, that is to say, may be a growth in wisdom and in self-understanding. Each human person is unique, and although throughout life we may become shock-ingly conscious that 'other people' fit categories and may be dreadfully predictable – shocking because in so many cases our instincts in this kind of assessment prove to be accurate – nevertheless we shall also see, if we are perceptive, that in each of us there is a personal code. God made us so, and our identity as individuals who are to endure forever is not set in relationship to our contemporaries, but to him. In the world, however, from which we derive both the conditioning of our natures and also our source of knowledge, we are unavoidably locked together in a society which is often not of our choosing. Part of the noble potential of our natures – quite a large part – comes from our acceptance of this. Then follows a creative celebration of our relationship with others to enhance the passage of life for them and for ourselves. But however sensitively and successfully these encounters are turned to good effect they are all, in the end, destined to extinction. There is, Jesus said, no marriage in heaven. Our lives are finite, at least in worldly terms, and our status is that of transients. Loneliness is a fact of existence, yet it can become a vocation if we choose to make it one. The interior isolation of the person can then be recognized as an anticipation of our exclusive ownership by God. The glory of the Christian religion is the mercy of God: that he did not leave his creatures alone in the vast dust of the universe, but offered us a personal relationship with him. He came into the world in the form of his Son, and he is in the world, still, in the body which is his Church. It is here that we may see the shadow cast by the illumination of the heavenly society, which beckons us from loneliness to the company of the blessed, from life to eternal life.

Seventy One

The star of Bethlehem

ℬℭ

Born in the lowliest of circumstances, but born, nevertheless, with the splendour of the heavenly bodies in attendance: the symbolism of the star which heralded the birth of Christ is very profound. It does not matter if it was a comet or some other natural phenomenon; it is the place of the star in signalling the truth about God and his creation which is important, and which is why the story has been treasured as part of the Christmas event. It is possible that Jesus was not even born in Bethlehem, and that the Gospel narrative has been made to correspond with the Davidic tradition in order to authenticate the claims of Jesus to be the Messiah. That, too, does not matter. It is the truth of Christ, and the symbolism in which it is received which should concern us – as it has concerned the millions in whose lives Jesus has been conveyed ever since. The ancients knew the stars well, and their learned men calculated according to the relationships of the celestial bodies. They may have been ignorant of the nature of the stars, in the way we no longer are, and they may have credited them with mystical meanings which were unwarranted – though this remains a feature of popular culture to this day. The important point, again, is not material but symbolical. Those who recorded the events accompanying the birth of Christ recognized that the whole universe was somehow involved: that here was an event unlike any other, which described something of the vastness and purpose of the whole creation. The stars themselves witnessed the nativity, God descended to the earth, and the world was made new. The miracle of the Incarnation was that

141

God chose to intervene in the lives of men and women. For he did not come into the world in order to effect a cosmic demonstration of his power, and Jesus scorned the value of 'signs and wonders'; he came in order to save those whom he regarded as his children. He had not set up the universe and then left it to proceed upon a course determined by the laws he had himself laid down. Those laws, it is true, are still the exclusive means by which all things are: but God involved himself personally. His physical laws remained, and applied to himself when he was on earth; what the birth of Christ indicated was the preparedness of God to *redeem* men and women. Their sins and corruptions, like the physical laws of creation, remained. What the coming of Christ gave was *forgiveness*. The star of Bethlehem drew the whole of the created universe into the great act of love; the heavenly bodies acknowledged the astonishing importance of the event. We like to see ourselves today as being the first to have authentic knowledge of the universe, and that is in its way obviously true. What we do not remember is that the ancient world, too, recognized how vast was the scale of creation, and how insignificant the phenomenon of human life. The star which pointed to the birth of Jesus linked our fate with the greater design of God.

Seventy Two

Forgiving past wrongs
෨෬

The year which is passing saw a number of events commem-
orating the warfare and associated atrocities which have
characterized our century. Societies all look back at their own
histories, and it is right that the definitive episodes and the
often legendary interpretations which get attached to them
provide a collective memory and a sense of national cohesion.
That is how societies achieve and preserve some sense of
common purpose, and add dignity and nobility to human
association. It is also right that the deaths of so many should
not go unremembered. But recent commemorations are subtly
different from their predecessors. There has been an increase of
the tendency – as yet only a straw in the wind – to employ
commemoration of past events to indoctrinate the young into
approved values which have an almost wholly modern
reference. Under other guises this has always to some extent
happened. The difference now is the means of using propaganda models drawn from the past which are considerably
more accessible and effective. There are those, on the other
hand, who believe that the dead should bury their dead. They
recognize that the wickedness of mankind is not exclusive to
particular groups, and that as long as the earth endures there
will be terrible human events. They believe that evil should
always be condemned, but that human depravity is a steady
state, and that the routine representation of past wrongs is not
the way to help men and women through the difficulties of the
present. Forgiveness implies wiping the slate clean; burying the
orchestrated remembrance of things which once stimulated

hatreds or were caused by them. For others, however – and they would appear to be growing in influence – the revival of dreadful memories instructs the young in approved attitudes and so will prevent recurrences. The past must be kept alive, not, they would argue, in order to cater to vindictiveness, but so that the world will learn lessons. The danger with this second approach, laudable though its motivation perhaps is, lies in its very understanding of the past. What is revived for commemoration, that is to say, has too much reference to the emotions of the present to be authentic or balanced history. The past is not really recalled: it is the propaganda needs of the present, represented as the authentic rediscovery of the meaning of events long gone. The ends served are not truth but present ideology – the demands of modern nationalism or modern politics, or modern moralism. The process is also necessarily selective: humanity acts badly all the time and in all cultures, and to represent one or another as peculiarly liable to wickedness will leave many others equally culpable out of the picture. Then the realities of the past are distorted and the moral capacities of the present made to appear more dependable than they are. Forgiveness costs a lot in personal terms, and it certainly involves the surrender of past hatreds. As the earth moves into another year, human society is unlikely to behave any differently – but it can at least benefit from the forgiving love of God.

Seventy Three

Liberation from sin

ಶೋಟ್ವ

The Christian life begins with contrition, an act of repentance, and the receipt of God's forgiveness. Many people, it is true, are put off Christianity because they find that the conduct of the forgiven is thereafter very little different from anyone else's. Hence the common charge of hypocrisy. But Christians have a realistic view of human nature. It is materialists who breezily dismiss the idea of inherent corruption, regarding men and women as morally autonomous creatures, whose faults are the product of unsatisfactory programming – an unavoidable effect of the diverse circumstances of life. Given ideal conditions, they suppose, humanity can be made, if not perfect, at least more socially adapted. That is why they have relied so much on the hope that if the cultural and material environment of men and women is changed, a better world will result. It is not a modern idea, but in our own century an almost pathetic mass utopianism has pervaded the political expectations of the world's peoples. It would be helpful to be able to say that the ideologies reflecting these assumptions – of which there have been several versions in the twentieth century – were all in turn rejected because people found their essential belief in the inherent reasonableness of mankind to be false: in fact they were all rejected because they failed to deliver material benefits. Thus Communism collapsed in eastern Europe not because of spiritual weariness with its materialist view of humanity, but because the disaffected élites who lived under it wanted the kind of material possessions commonplace among the consumers of Western society. Subtler renditions of

---

145

materialism are still only too freely available. They are taught in the classrooms of most schools in the Western world at this moment, and take the form of regarding ideological precision as bigoted 'dogma' and directing children, instead, to 'caring', or material welfare, as the basis of 'higher' attitudes to the life of mankind. It is a kind of parody of Christian virtue. Christianity actually rejects materialism absolutely. What is wrong with men and women is not an accident of their upbringing and material circumstances but of their very natures. They are creatures in rebellion against their Creator, and they have usurped his sovereignty to order the earth as they will. At the centre of their beings is a bias to depravity, and it survives all their attempts at amendment – so that the need of God's forgiveness is perpetual. Modern people don't feel very much as if they have sinned: it is one of the oldest characteristics of men and women to recognize evil but not to identify their own conduct as part of it. Somehow we always find exceptions for ourselves. We believe ourselves to be the best judges of ourselves. Our errors are not really errors – they are the consequences of the actions of others. And so forth. It was to such people, to people like us, that Jesus came and offered the love which earned only his death. The serenity of his presence, and his act of forgiveness, are forever available to us. He still stands at the door of our hearts, and we have only to let him in.

Seventy Four

Sin

ॐ

There is not much emphasis today on the dreadful reality of human sin. Where once the pulpits sounded forth about individual wickedness, about the frailty of our nature, about the need for repentance, now there is much more likely to be a call for social justice, or ecological responsibility. These issues of our present concern are all very important, and it is doubtless necessary to call our attention to them; but they are of the earth, and the prior fact of human sin requires an emphasis it is not getting if we are to transcend the earthly and glimpse the heavenly. The present debate about crime, in all Western countries, makes the concept of human wickedness a familiar one – but it is located in a specialist manner, which demonizes others but leaves the sin of each individual uncondemned. Certain people are identified as criminal; they are contrasted with 'decent people'. The sins of the criminal are not historically stable: each moment of time appears to contrive its own list of wrongdoing. In the last century, for example, various sexual practices were regarded as unspeakable fornication. Today they are considered quite normal or even healthy. We, for our part, are horrified by a rapidly changing succession of wickedness whose evidences are supplied by the chance of publicity. One year the worst we can imagine is rape; the next it is child abuse; when everything else has been used up there is always glue-sniffing among the young. Sin is a familiar concept in our society, but it has become something done by other people in television documentaries.

Jesus said he came into the world for sinners. He came for *all* of us, that is to say. We need to restore the sense of human moral inadequacy, to redefine ourselves as creatures unavoidably inseparable from our lower natures, who stand in need of God's forgiveness. We confirm our false assumption of moral self-confidence by drawing caricatures of past moral censure – when the pulpits were supposed to have resonated with ignorant (and perhaps prurient) condemnation, and when ordinary people were subjected to the moral tyranny of priests who were agents of a social control prescribed by the ruling classes.

In a Christian perspective, however, the worst sins are spiritual, not moral, and they are found evenly spread throughout all of us. They are things like doubting the providence of God, rejecting his sovereignty in our lives, or putting material above spiritual priorities. Thus we marginalize the concept of sin itself when we exult moral failures above religious ones. It hardly needs to be said that the current list of conventional sins is to do with criminal behaviour rather than with wrong belief. Most people today, for example, would regard child abuse as worse than atheism. They are content to regard criminals as 'beasts', unlike themselves. But sin is evenly distributed, and it reaches the same levels in every age and among all people. Men and women stand in need of God's forgiveness; what is wrong with us is out of all possibility of self-correction – and it is *we* who are the sinners, not somebody else.

Seventy Five

———

Ascended and glorified

ॐ

Christianity is centred in trust. We are called to trust in God and in his providential arrangement, both of the circumstances of our lives and of the world in which we live 'and have our being'. But it is precisely this sort of trust that modern people find extremely difficult. We are beset with anxieties, and life for many becomes choked by preoccupation with security. Those who expect so much, and who believe themselves entitled to so much, are incapable of dealing with the normal hazards and uncertainties of life. No matter how hard we try to protect ourselves against fate we find ourselves subject to it: loved ones leave us or die, fearful disease or age itself reduces our independence, our children are ungrateful, jobs and homes are lost. Most of the things which afflict us, in fact, are not susceptible to human solution whatever we do. For the world as God has made it was not designed for our comfort and convenience: we are creatures placed in an environment whose providential purposes are not known to us. God in his mercy has regard for our fate, yet we in our ingratitude rail against him for not having given us immunity from the way the creation works. Even the environment itself is now a subject of human complaint: how can God have afflicted us with so much sorrow? Some – and it is an increasing number – find themselves unable to believe in the reality of a God whose world so persistently interrupts our pursuit of a painless existence. They cannot see that it is we who have made demands beyond our place in the creation, who expect special treatment not available to the buzzing mass of living tissues that cover the face of the planet. God has raised us to consciousness and to a measure of creativity; we ignore the graciousness of the gift and claim the benefits of divinity for ourselves.

It is hardly surprising, therefore, that men and women have problems also with trusting in religious tradition, for it is something not within our immediate capacity to verify. Religious truth, to be known about, depends upon trusting others. This last week the Christian world celebrated the Ascension of Christ. It was an event that seems at variance with the expectations of the prevailing material culture, and scepticism about its historical reality will have been voiced in quite a number of pulpits: it is common these days to interpret the miracle in a non-literal sense. But Christians are dependent for a knowledge of the historical truth of the Ascension on the same body of preceding believers whose witness and testimony has authenticated all other aspects of Christianity. They know about the truth of the Resurrection from the same source. To interpret either event in symbolical or metaphorical style is at variance with the record of the Faith itself, and is anyway quite unnecessary. To trust in God is to trust in a miraculous presence – not, perhaps, in the everyday passage of events, but in the grand design which is expressed in the world and which provides the true environment of our lives rather than the shadows which pass.

Seventy Six

Whitsun Eve

ೲඋ

When people talk about the Church they inevitably refer to it as an institution. They see it as a fellowship of believers, a gathering for worship, the venue of good works, a place of spiritual refreshment. When they say that so-and-so 'left the Church' or, perhaps more rarely, 'joined' the Church, it is a personal habit that is described. Church buildings themselves were once seen as the focus of community, and the Church of England still trains its clergy to regard the fostering of community consciousness as a central dimension of ministry; it is a short step to defining the Church in terms of its institutional form. Even when people recognize – as Sunday school children used to be taught – that the Church is 'the people and not the building', they may still persist in identifying the essential function of the Church as its utility. It is then seen as a society of believers dedicated to morally elevating purposes. In these sad days, when the exaltation of humanity and its needs has achieved priority, and is the highest good that can be imagined, the Church tends to be thought of as a place for personal uplift, a therapy facility, the corporate expression of ideals which will give significance to the lives of adherents.

The Church founded by Jesus Christ, in its traverse of time, may indeed gather up some of these characteristics: it can only address the world when it shares some of the world's expectations. The Church also has to be an institution, since Christ committed his truth to a living tradition of believers, and not to a book, or a school of philosophy, or a sect of initiates. It needs officers and teachers, and it needs the financial resources which can maintain a presence in society. But the Church only lends itself to institutional expression: it is not of its nature an institution. For it is the very body of Christ in the world, the mystical presence of the Saviour, the exclusive means of salvation. Who would know the mind of Christ must resort to its teachings, and who would seek the forgiveness of sins will find there the arms of the Lord himself open in reception and greeting to the penitent. Whitsun is the celebration of truth, of the gift of the Holy Spirit who, as Christ promised, would preserve his people in all truth. The eternal message and the everlasting blessing of God himself are thus conveyed to sinful men and women by others who are themselves no less sinful, yet who are marked by their submission to the governance of Christ. That is the splendour of Christianity: all people, in their degrees of corruption and virtue, and in their different capacities for understanding or moral consistency, can be incorporated into the body of Jesus. It is his sacred heart which sustains the action of their allegiance to the author of all things, and it is his love which enables the least in the societies of the world to become the greatest in the kingdom of heaven. The Church viewed as an institution is full of human failings. As the conveyance of Christ, however, it is celestial splendour translated into the world of people like us.

Seventy Seven

A glimpse into the inferno

ೞೞೞ

The idea of enhancing the quality of human life, and of preventing some sorts of avoidable human suffering, by manipulating the genes, is not in itself theologically alien. God called men and women to share with him in the work of creation – which the Bible consistently depicts as a continuing process. We were endowed with the faculties of reason and reflection, which enable the exploration of the nature of things and a philosophical contemplation of the meaning and order of the creation. It is, indeed, the only dignity attaching to human life that God himself raised us from the dust and made himself known to us. Through the use of intellect, and after observation of our place in the creative processes, we employed practical and scientific knowledge to improve the nature of human life. This was not just a matter of self-interest: the alleviation of bodily suffering, and the provision of material benefits, were allied to moral understanding. These things were accomplished in the light of ideas about ourselves and our creator. It was a *moral* act to help another out of suffering, and it was in honour of the beneficence and greatness of God that men probed the mysteries of the universe. Western culture had a religious basis. It is only in our own day that the union of knowledge and discovery with morality and spiritual integrity has fallen apart; it is only in the past couple of centuries that a race emancipated (as it has imagined itself to be) from outmoded cosmology has come to exercise autonomy in the use of the resources of the earth.

The fearful problem about gene therapy is the unstated object of designer human beings – the attempt to produce people without blemishes, both in terms of their physical condition and of their social behaviour. For already, before the science has scarcely had time to establish itself, some of its technicians are beginning to speak of identifying and eliminating genes which might lead to violence, or to what are thought of as errant sexuality. Who decides what is appropriate in this proposed process of elimination, and what the moral or religious frame of reference is in which it is to take place? The question is only addressed by medical or legislative advisory bodies – so-called 'ethical committees' – whose moral pragmatism is well established, and who are therefore in reality as much at sea in these uncharted waters as the laymen seeking guidance. A truly chilling future is opening up, especially since the only effective way of eliminating some genes is actual abortion. Now that the co-discoverer of DNA himself has pointed to the possibility of allowing women to abort babies who may turn out to be homosexual, the whole issue is before the public in a very stark manner. Knowing what aspects of the creation God himself intends us to regard as permanent, and what aspects are transient, was never going to be easy, and it calls for all our resources of scholarship and moral understanding. The ethical illiteracy of this generation makes it the least suited to perform the task. The result will be majority decisions about basic issues of human life. It is a bleak future indeed.

Seventy Eight

Service

ࡥ࠰ࡩ

It is possible that you can judge the temper of an age by the degree of altruism its people exhibit. Is there a prevailing ideology which encourages virtues that are of no direct benefit to those who possess them? Are the young taught the obligations of service, and that putting the interests of others before their own is a higher objective than self-gratification? Are personal possessions held in a kind of trust, or are they valued as indications of status or the sources of individual pleasure? Of course our lives in the world were meant to afford occasions of enjoyment, and a puritanism which failed to recognize that individuals become better people through a total experience of a range of what the world can offer would be confining indeed. But ours is an age of selfishness. Children in our schools are in fact encouraged to cultivate 'self-esteem'; they are brought up to see the emotions as the providers of pleasure and entertainment, and are even outraged by the presentation of reality as suffering or deprivation. The young today, even in the poorest families, possess so much compared with their predecessors – and with most of the rest of the world. What is now defined as poverty in Western societies is somebody else's luxury. This is not to justify gross differentials in the social well-being of society, nor to foster ignorance about the need for change where that is appropriate or necessary. But it is to shake us out of the appalling deadweight of personal absorption with material things: the concentration on ourselves and our entitlements. We seem to think that token 'concern' for randomly presented occasions of suffering among other

155

people, perhaps in some distant land or some far-off city, is an indication of genuine altruism. We also seem to believe that the sensations derived from worship at the shrine of 'the arts' are somehow, in themselves, ennobling and spiritualizing. Even the word 'spiritual', incidentally, is today often used in a wholly secular sense to mean virtually anything which elevates the emotions. Behind our self-absorption lies very little; we live for immediate gratification of the senses, for entertainment, for the cultivation of ourselves. It is hardly surprising that in such a society people see so little point in obligations to others, when those obligations can seem no more than an irksome intrusion upon our pursuit of self-fulfilment. So marriage partners break up their relationship if either feels it inhibits personal aspirations, and people in general experience no sense of a higher dimension in the ideals of personal service to others.

Christianity, in contrast, has always viewed the life of man as conditional: God made promises to those who undertake obligations – and the first obligation is the surrender of self, the recognition that sinful natures are incapable of self-correction. We are not in the world to luxuriate in our own interests but to serve God through the service of others. It is an ideal few of us can live up to, yet it must remain the ideal.

Seventy Nine

The self-remedy that fails

೫಄ಌ

Perhaps the greatest suffering that can be experienced is to observe the suffering of others – especially when they are ill. Sickness is so common, and as life is prolonged more and more (in developed societies) the progressive decay of old age is marked by frequent lapses into ill-health. Very many of us will pass from vitality to dependence, as our bodies are kept going by medical skills and our spirits are wearied by too long an experience of the world. Thus infirmity is becoming normal. We need to remember that when Jesus healed the sick he was concerned for people whose lives were relatively short, and who were anyway the healthier survivals of high infant mortality. His ministry, that is to say, was among those whose lives were in their most productive stage: they were healed so that they might proceed with the everyday labour around them, to fulfil earthly tasks which enabled them to make a contribution to the society they lived in. With us, on the other hand, it is geriatric illness which is now the most common – despite the fact that older people are becoming healthier – simply because of the lengthening of life. Hence the double sorrow of observing not only the pains of illness but the sense of uselessness which those experience who are marginalized by age from the energy of life around them. To be granted a prolonged existence only to have its quality and purpose snatched away is galling enough; the frustration of social redundancy combined with actual ill-health is a truly heavy cross to have to bear. It is a major problem of our times, whose future implications – if they are considered at all – should cause great unease.

Christians, however, are not called into the world in order to despair: their belief in Providence does not answer questions or resolve material problems, but it does set things in a wider context. So many of our anxieties, and the causes of our suffering, are self-inflicted. Life has been prolonged by human action; it is human decisions which have led to the medical and social advances by which individual lives are extended, and it is human skills which produce the ambiguous advantages of longevity. Christians believe that they are acting in correspondence with divine intentions when they practise the knowledge which, in theory at least, improves the condition of living. For they are sharing with God in the creative processes. Unhappily, in a sort of cosmic reminder of the essential frailty of our natures, we are forever defeated in our ultimate objectives. Human life is indeed prolonged, but so often at the price of its quality – anxiety about an early death is replaced by the horrors of geriatric dependence. Some illness can be cured, by the same God-given skills; the capacity to do so, however, merely encourages people in the belief that they are entitled to a painless existence. Our solutions produce more problems, and our claims to benefits in life slip out of control. Christ did not come into this world of dreadful suffering in order to change its nature, but in order to redeem it.

Eighty

Love of strangers

୫ଠଓଃ

Most of us think that life would be fine if it wasn't for the irritating behaviour of other people, and most of us, too, recognize that we can't get on without others. It is part of the daily tension of existence. Wise people look into their own natures in order to identify, and if possible to correct, those traits of personality which prompt irritation in others. Most of us, alas, simultaneously retain a sense that we are, essentially, good and decent individuals whose ways are misunderstood. The self-critical faculties, that is to say, operate within limitations. And it remains one of the most trying features of life that our motives are frequently misinterpreted: even the words we use convey different resonances as they are received by others. People believe what they want to believe, and they hear what they want to hear. The remarkable thing about human society is that we communicate as effectively as we do.

Now Christians may be able to assist understanding – in this attrition of personalities – if they reflect upon one aspect of our natures that really does unite us: our sinfulness. Since, in the perspective of religion, no one is exempted from the earthiness of our natures, all share a common need of reconciliation to God. It helps, for example, when walking down a street or waiting in a queue, to offer a silent prayer for the people you pass or see. Anonymous and unknown they are yet God's children, co-inhabitants of the territory of the morally frail and the spiritually flawed. Ask God to give them light, and ask the same for yourself. If we pray only for those we know our prayers will be very narrowly based. But routinely praying for people we don't know can be of enormous service, for it will inevitably include those who do not pray for themselves, and who therefore especially need our prayers. Look at the haunting faces in press photographs of criminals: made in God's image, here are people whom the world rejects because of their weaknesses, and who, again, especially need our prayers. In this case the most appropriate prayer is not that they should come to fit in with society's understanding of acceptable behaviour, but that Christ will be with them – extending, as the Saviour does to everyone, the hand of support and the love which promises forgiveness. A prayer becomes a means of communication, not a tariff of personal demands. Unseen and unrecognized in the crowd, prayer for another is a translation of the shared sinfulness of men and women to the place of forgiveness; if universally practised it would establish a silent communion of enormous power. Jesus commended the man who went into the Temple to pray and called upon God to help a confessed sinner. He did not condemn the other man, of conventional piety, but observed that he had exhausted his virtues and had his reward. Our prayers are too often conventional petitions, when they might engage the service of those who most need our prayers.

Eighty One

The enemy within

ಬಿಂ

There are some exceptions, but in most parts of the world intellectual opinion supports the religion which is part of its historic culture. Thus in Islamic countries the schools and universities are plainly sympathetic to Islam, and indeed actively promote it. In India, especially in the current revival of Hindu fundamentalism, Hindu beliefs are treated with respect – and in a country, furthermore, whose constitution is formally secular. It is only in the Christian West that intellectual opinion is broadly hostile, or indifferent, to its own religious tradition. This is, in fact, one of the ways (and there are others) in which Western societies are subverting their own values. Now we in the West have become exponents of the concept of plural values, and the difficulty for us is that the liberal advantages inherent in this seem inseparable from a withdrawal of official support for religious belief. We no longer wish to use educational institutions or the authority of the state to propagate Christianity. In some countries, as in England and Scotland, with their residual links of Church and state, there are surviving traces of state endorsement of belief, but the reality is that it is 'Christian values', understood in the most diluted form, which receive recognition and not the Christian religion as a doctrinal structure. For most practical purposes, and increasingly, this is a secular state. The state schools do not instruct in religious belief as once they did, but offer the children a range of knowledge about all religions, in order that they may be acquainted with them as cultural phenomena. We regard this as satisfactory because it allows that element of liberal choice which is very properly a part of our national outlook.

The result is not objectivity, however. What actually happens in our schools is the promotion of secular ethicism, often with the support of teachers who regard themselves as Christian. In the absence of a coherent moral alternative to the received Christian deposit of ideas, a sort of hedonistic creed is taught. The end is seen to be human happiness, the means to self-development of the individual person, and the machinery for the moralizing of society is the concept of 'caring'. Moral good is perceived as helping the unfortunate and punishing the deviant. It is a sort of lowest common denominator presented as the highest insight of human development. It amounts, in the end, to the propagation of materialist humanism. 'Spiritual' values are identified as elevated human sentiments, and the movement of the senses by aesthetic appreciation. In the universities and colleges Christianity is being relativized, by an intellectual culture which assumes that religious belief may be explained in wholly human terms. There are, of course, genuine intellectual advances to be gained by doing this, but as a definitive account of the nature of religious insights it is, to say the least, defective. There is no mystery about the creeping secularization of our day: it derives from lost habit and the loss of a basis for religious instruction in education. But the new secularism has no name, no philosophical school by which to identify it. It is the thief in the night, and is, accordingly, all the more insidious.

Eighty Two

The emptiness within

໔ໆ

Very many people in our society – probably most people – live
fairly blameless lives, behave decently towards others, avoid
occasions of wrongdoing, look after those who are dependent
upon them. They are untroubled by 'higher' reflections about
the nature and purpose of human existence, and such issues as
whether humanity is inherently capable of self-improvement,
or whether men and women are by nature internally corrupt,
are not likely to disturb them greatly. Ours is a society driven
not by profound visions of life, but by 'issues': we are
concerned with crime, conservation of the environment, the
enhancement of human capabilities, the management of
welfare. What are thought of as higher dimensions of human
life are sought in the cultivation of individual sensibilities – an
appreciation of the arts, perhaps, or moral concern about the
material fate of people who are left behind in the otherwise
unashamed pursuit of well-being. Religion comes into the
scene, to the extent that it comes in at all, as another dimension
of human self-enrichment. It is regarded as a benign presence
in life, a therapy, a set of beautiful reflections which will assist
personal significance and possibly instil a sense of 'values' in
the young. As such, religion is at the margin of daily living –
even for those who believe themselves to be believers. Societies
in which religious conviction is allowed to interfere with the
routine arrangements of existence are judged fanatical or
sectarian: places like the Islamic states or Northern Ireland.
Worldly priorities, that is to say, have won hands down in
Western societies in general. We regard human material welfare

as more important than ultimate beliefs: an extraordinary reversal of the preceding history of human endeavour. We regard the liberal dogma of choice as more valuable than what is actually chosen – unless, of course, it conflicts with prevalent secular pieties.

Now it would be distressing to return to conditions of intolerance and absence of choice; and the modern world has gained much. But individual lives are not so much impoverished by the avoidance of religious reference as rendered meaningless. It seems that the more material problems we solve, and the more humanity becomes capable of manipulating the circumstances of existence, the less we are able to recognize an overriding purpose to things. It was a condition actually known to the ancients, too, and the fear of chaos – by which they meant spiritual chaos – is something we could learn from them. Society is increasingly ordered and regulated in a manner which may in due course produce a truly fearful lack of individual freedom. This makes the internal liberation of which religious belief is an indication even more necessary. The lives of men and women who are unacquainted with reference to a sovereign outside of themselves, and with arrangements representing higher purposes than those put in place by governments, are barren indeed. It is of the essence of religious belief that men and women become the agents of the divine will.

Eighty Three

———

Healing with a purpose

ℬℭ

It is St Luke's day, a traditional occasion for offering prayers for medical work, under the patronage of Luke the Physician. In the modern world the terms of reference for the morality of medicine are now so changed that it is difficult to recall the simple association which people once made between the great love of God and the compassionate practice of healing: an association consecrated by the actions of Christ himself, and forming a noble and continuing tradition in the Churches. It is now changed in two major ways. First, medical technology has made men and women capable of manipulating the substance of life itself, and in directions which have no preceding moral guidelines. Secondly, people in modern society are progressively given to regarding health provision as a kind of substitute for religion. It is a characteristic of a materialist culture, for example, that physical good done to people is more important than what they believe – in a philosophical or spiritual sense. In our society it is not the priest or the thinker who is the hero, but the nurse and the carer. There is some positive good in this: it is a delight to see those who seek to alleviate the sufferings of others rewarded with public esteem. But there are also disadvantages, not least of which is the barbarous priority of placing material welfare above spiritual truth. Can we not have both? In some that is indeed accomplished. Yet the problem of the modern world is that medical advance has chanced to occur simultaneously with the collapse of spiritual certainties. 'Ethical' committees set up to monitor, and even sometimes to determine, issues involving the most fundamental interferences with the nature of human life operate without any real measure of philosophical agreement beyond a vague humanism. Their sovereign principles, as a result, depend upon largely rhetorical declamations about the value of human life: there is no coherent philosophical basis, no external authority of moral ideas to which reference can be made. It is not the purpose of human existence which enters the calculations, but the welfare of humanity in a material sense. The result is a lack of clarity now, and a mass of problems stacking up for the future as techniques become ever more effective.

So behind the familiar shambles of the television panel debating some matter of medical advance, there is the simple phenomenon of philosophical atrophy and spiritual decline. Most of the medical advances are good; most of the extensions of human capabilities are actually demonstrations of men and women joining with the divine will in the development of the planet and the life it sustains. But the philosophical void is foolishness; so is the absence of urgency in trying to give a systematic basis for the ethics of the 'ethical' committees. St Luke's day symbolizes the union of healing and spirituality. Shall we strive to restore it?

Eighty Four

All Saints

ᏇᏬᏗ

It is All Saints Day today. And who is a saint? The complexity of our natures makes none of us simply good or simply bad: we are the consequences of too many conditions over which we have no control. Each person is formed by genetic determination, infant experience, and acquired ideas. The disposition to structured behaviour finds its expression in an enormous number of alternatives, and the definition of goodness or badness attached to particular modes of behaviour shows a high degree of relative judgement through time and culture. In one age a man is accounted good, for example, because he seeks the punishment of those who spread opinions regarded erroneous or vicious by the prevailing culture; in another he is condemned for lack of liberalism or tolerance. We are determined in so many ways, and our minds are opened to alternatives in such an arbitrary and piecemeal fashion, that it must sometimes seem hopeless to try to isolate definitions of authentic goodness. Modern knowledge has exposed the nuts and bolts of the human psyche; the decay of an agreed basis for ethical value has robbed us of certainties about the estimates we should make of our own conduct.

But sanctity is not actually about goodness – at least in the ordinary sense society now understands. The saint is the one who tries to transcend his nature, or to use its ambiguous directives for spiritual formation. Thus sanctity begins with self-awareness, and in a universally fallen creation that means awareness of sin. That is why the teaching of Jesus began with a call to repentance. No one can be recognized as a Christian, least of all a saint, who does not regularly confess sin and ask for forgiveness. While in the world, however, we continue to be conditioned by our natures, and the attempts at sanctity – at transcending our circumstance – will be partial. Saints may be people who are not capable of overall goodness, but whose lives in one or more dimensions of spirituality achieve insight and expression. To the eyes of the world they may seem unpromising candidates for holiness. Jesus was censured in his day for consorting with sinners, some of whom, in responding to his call, became truly saints. Doubtless in many things their lives remained unreconstructed, and to the conventional their spiritual aspirations must have seemed negligible. But not to God. It still shocks people today to be told that Jesus loves child-molesters and murderers, and criminals may even achieve sanctity if in other dimensions of their nature they seek submission to the will of God and amend their lives. Those whom the Lord calls to spiritual awareness are not transformed in the whole of their humanity. The corruption in their natures endures; it is their attempts at personal transcendence which furnish the materials of the spiritual life. Who is a saint? Saints are people like us, people who try to see God. Any simple goodness we acquire in the process is merely a by-product.

Eighty Five

Death wish

ଥ୦ଓଃ

A person's attitude to death relates a great deal about how he sees life. It is actually very instructive that when someone is asked for their response to the death of a well-known public figure their reply inevitably conveys the state of their feelings rather than an evaluation of the unfortunate deceased. Thus the first reaction is not 'he was a very great man', or whatever, but 'I was shocked', or 'I felt devastated'. Death is in this sense an indicator of egocentricity: the value of life is measured by the extent to which it affects our personal emotions. The death of a celebrity, therefore, becomes the occasion for excessive self-dramatizing, an indulgence which is perhaps harmless enough in itself but which encourages a kind of pseudo-reality in which the self is made the arbiter of all things. The control of grief is like the pursuit of happiness, or any other human emotional impulse: its indulgence is bad for spiritual health. It is also true that dramatizing death allows a market for the manufacture of myth. So often the qualities that are attributed to a person at death were not really possessed by them but are simply conventional pieties of the age. This, too, is probably harmless in itself, but is an offence against truth. It also operates both ways. Celebrities or public figures create a propaganda image for public consumption in their lifetime, and if observers choose to take that at face value, and to enhance it with the mystique of death, so be it. The history of human society is full of fairly worthless people who achieved fame by such means – these days some are assisted by expensive professional consultants. Yet it is as well to remember that those accounted corrupt or evil at the time of their demise may actually have been possessed of spiritual or personal qualities which the world's consensus did not see. The greater the integrity of a person the less likely it is that they will parade their qualities to achieve recognition in their lifetime. It was the man who went into the Temple to pray and who confessed himself a sinner, rather than the virtuous man who declaimed his virtue, who was commended by Christ.

Death should be the occasion of remembering that we are all in the end very similar – given to human failings, limited by our natures, sometimes striving for self-improvement, always ambiguous in our motives. It used to be the great virtue of the Anglican Funeral Service that it was the same for everyone; the cool words of the Prayer Book reminding us of the wretchedness of human achievement and the supervening mercy of God. Today, characteristically, mourners like to personalize funerals, using the service as an occasion to eulogize their loved ones, and expunging, as far as they are able, mention of death itself. And so they are robbed of a most significant moment to set existence into a realistic context. We are given life as a gift; we leave the earth with an added value that is known only to God.

Eighty Six

———

An intimidating new world

ଽଠ୯ଽ

As the century draws to its end there are two worrying features of public life which require more critical scrutiny than they sometimes attract. One is increasing regulation of people's lives by the state; the other is the manipulation of opinion. Both, characteristically, are phenomena which are so wrapped up in familiar euphemisms, and presented as moral advance, that they are acceptable to a public which has no overview, no set of references by which to judge them. Both, also, have been around for a long time. 'Totalitarian' government in the 1930s practised the arts of state control and propaganda (today called 'news management') with what now seems a breathtaking frankness. They were supposed to have been purged – the European Fascist examples through warfare, the Communist ones by internal collapse. But their reappearance, in acceptable and benign modes, is made all the more sinister because of their anonymity: they are not attached to identifiable political creeds, and they are assisted by the revolution in technology which makes social control to a high degree effective. The computer and the television screen are so much a part of daily life, and offer so many benefits, that we do not worry about their Orwellian implications.

The extension of state control has paradoxically occurred at a time when Western governments had proclaimed that they were 'rolling back the frontiers of the state'. State power is now exercised through intermediate agency – 'regulation'. But

171

though disguised, it is nevertheless just government managing increasingly refined details of individual lives. A mother, for example, who goes off and leaves her child unattended for an afternoon is not just a bad mother: she is prosecuted and the child 'taken into care' (i.e. seized by the state). And here is the key to the process. This is done in the name of agreed moral good – and so, perhaps, it is. But large areas of morality were always intended to be enforced by individual choice and the sanction of conscience. The enfolding structure of 'regulation' is beginning to constitute a kind of substitute moral system, compulsion without a philosophical basis except a vague welfare humanism. The manipulation of opinion, comparably, is not according to a recognizable ideology, but is in the interests of 'decency' and populist moral virtue. Again, it is centred in supposedly agreed moral good. Its manifestations are episodic and sometimes dramatic: as in the creation of mass opinion in attitudes to criminals, or the allocation of blame after a disaster, or the engineering of what are claimed to be spontaneous expressions of grief at the death of a celebrity. Those actually doing the manipulation are difficult to identify, and do not constitute a coherent class or social section. Hence the ease with which what has come to be called 'political correctness' has been intruded. Christianity is addressed to the individual soul and it calls for individual response. So often in the past people nevertheless adopted or discarded it collectively, as a cultural facet of their social state. Modern liberal individualism, and freedom of choice in moral judgement and religion, has offered men and women a real advance. Let it not be laid aside now, in an unconscious surrender to mass conditioning.

Eighty Seven

Changing times

‮ဆ‬

There is widespread consciousness of the decline of religious belief and observance in Western societies; Pope John Paul II spoke of it at the time of the Paris rally for young people in August of this year. What is less noticed is the extent to which the Christian recession is not leaving a void but is being replaced by something else. The difficulty is that the replacement does not have a name by which it can be identified, nor does it have a systematic basis or a coherent statement of its principles. It is a collection of moral declamations. It is centred not on God but on humanity and its needs. Christianity is about the sovereignty of God and obedience owed to him; its replacement is about the welfare of men and women. Christianity makes demands about individual spiritual formation and the requirement of a disciplined life; its replacement is hedonistic, allowing all kinds of licence in the 'private' lives of individuals but imposing strict moral attitudes in social and welfare issues. Christianity is about forgiveness; its replacement seeks the punishment and correction of those who offend against right conduct. Christianity is, or ought to be, dogmatic – it rests upon precise statements of belief, and because the Church is the body of Christ in the world it needs to be very exacting in what is declared in his name. It is the voice of Christ himself who speaks through his earthly representatives. Its replacement, in another contrast, is not greatly exercised about ultimate beliefs, but puts the material well-being of men and women above religious convictions.

This emerging religion of secular humanism, which is often

popularly identified as applied Christianity, but is actually applied materialism, is producing its own saints. These are people of acknowledged moral virtue, not in their private lives – which are often accepted as being messy – but in their concern for the afflicted or in their devotion to good causes. They are the role model of the carers, and their sanctification most typically occurs in the wards of hospitals or in the stations of the emergency services. These are places, incidentally, which are glamorized and sentimentalized in television entertainment series, and fulfil the sort of heroic function which the mission field and the monastic cloister once provided in the lives of authentic saints. Much good undoubtedly derives from the succour encouraged by the religion of humanity. Its dark side, however, is its ignorance of the dark side of humanity itself, its impatience with ideological formulations, its appeal to false expectations about the capacity for human improvement, and its evocation of a species of moral tyranny – it is extremely intolerant of unbelievers and of its own heretics. It is also, in general, unforgiving.

Christianity, on the other hand, is addressed to sinners. Christ did not, on his own testimony, come for the righteous, and of the conventionally good he observed simply that they had their reward. Jesus is the Saviour of the morally inadequate, of the impure, of those who can't cope, of child-molesters and rapists, of the uncertain, of those who know what they ought to do but somehow don't have the strength to do it. His hand of pity is extended to such as these, as well as to the moral and correct people – who, if anything, will not feel the need to reach out and grasp it.

Eighty Eight

At the year's end

࿔

In the dying days of a year people's thoughts often touch upon the significance of time itself. Another year passes, and its events, both public and personal, descend to the sediment of accumulating memory, sometimes with regret, occasionally with relief. It is as well to remember that God himself works through time, and that our consciousness of his presence in the perpetual sequences of temporal change is important in our response to the purposes of existence. God works through time in the sense that the creation was a definable event: it did not occur through some gradual coincidence of influences, for all our modern knowledge seems to indicate a single and dramatic happening. The universe began and expanded, and persists in expansion, and time is the indicator of its progress. Now the Bible, and the words of Christ himself, are clear that the end, comparably, will be a single event. By 'end' is meant human life, reality as understood in relation to human habitation of the earth. Scriptural teaching also indicates that this will be some shocking cataclysm, perhaps like the one which ended the occupation of the world by the dinosaurs. Then the planet seems to have been coated with the debris of a collision with material from space. The earth itself endured, with some of its life-forms, but was regenerated in a different mode, with us as a consequence. God can make all things new. The end of the world – our world – may not therefore be the end of the planet as such, but only the end of the human race. 'In those days,' Christ is recorded as saying, in St Mark's Gospel, 'the sun shall be darkened, and the moon shall not give her light; and the stars of heaven shall fall.' The dreadful day which witnessed the demise of the dinosaurs must have been just such a time; and time, or the movement of materials in space, may yet, in the divine scheme, provide the occasion for the last account of humanity. Christians should live their lives as if that moment is imminent.

Taking stock of time is thus a Christian imperative. It enables a daily audit of our personal use of time – whether we have been profligate with such a precious commodity, or whether we have expended enough of it in the service of God's purposes. It is a strange paradox that in an age like ours, when men and women seek to prolong life, there is less and less awareness of any serious purpose to it. Individual lives have become a pursuit of security and happiness; time is an irritating impediment, an unwelcome reminder of personal decay. Christians are those who perceive an extremely serious purpose both to life and to time. It is nothing less than spiritual formation, converting the ingredients of life into the durable substance of participation with providence, to deploy qualities which have about them the materials of eternity. This goes against many of the common assumptions of humanity, for it is to deny the world's priorities and to reach out into the unfathomable purposes of God.

Eighty Nine

The end of life

೫೦೦೩

For many people life is a nexus of injustices. At the simplest level their motives are misunderstood or misrepresented by others, or the good they try to do somehow rebounds and produces negative consequences. In another remove, their lives are marked by opportunities which ought to have opened up but didn't, or their talents and hard work go unrewarded when others seem to forge ahead in the stakes of worldly success. Children show ingratitude after years dedicated to their upbringing; marriage partners, or partners, desert, or perhaps cruellest of all, a life-long search for someone to love proves barren. It is possible, indeed it is common, that after years of providing for security some upheaval of the market, or whatever, robs people of their protection in old age. Sickness has a very random incidence, and people today are convinced that health is a kind of entitlement: they are wrong in this but their feeling is real enough as a cause of a sense of injustice. Death itself, particularly when it visits a partner or a close family relation, is railed against in a society which does not know how to cope with it. Above all, as time delivers us into old age, life as a whole can be seen to have been a disappointment, an assemblage of unfulfilled ambitions and unrecognized effort.

These are all, however, attitudes of our own contrivance. We do not need to feel injustice. In objective terms our treatment at the hands of fate, or of others, is certainly often unfair – but we are people, not objects, and it is *our* choice when we estimate the world as a catalogue of the benefits which will fall to us. Of course less worthy people than ourselves flourish – less worthy in our own definition, and perhaps really so by some absolute standard. One certain thing is that it is not the virtuous but self-publicists and the well-connected who inherit the earth. So what? The earth may not be particularly well managed in their custody, but the worth of the individual who beholds it is not affected. The truth is that life does not owe us anything except the chance to use out time in the cultivation of spiritual consciousness. And in that task, as the teaching of Jesus makes clear in, for example, the Sermon on the Mount, there is a kind of reversal of conventional expectations. It is the marginalized and the insignificant who achieve authentic insight, and the successful and powerful who are left with little but success and power. The essential part of us, the part of us which is to survive, that is to say, has no worldly tests by which it is recognized: it is the part which has the quality called 'eternal'. Eternal life starts in life; it is life used productively in the individual work of spiritual formation. If our expectations are determined by a desire for worldly recognition, or happiness, or security, or release from pain, then we shall be disappointed. If they are fixed by our determination to glimpse the evidences of the unseen world in the debris of our human hopes they have a realistic chance of delivering us into an eternal life which extends far beyond our experience of earthly society. 'Come to me, all you who labour,' Jesus said, 'and I will give you rest.'

Ninety

The Resurrection of
Christ

ℬℭ

Public opinion polls appear to show that more people believe
in personal reincarnation than in the Resurrection of Jesus,
and that very many people claim to believe in both. It is not a
very encouraging finding. Nor is the growing tendency among
Christians to interpret the Resurrection as a symbolical rather
than an actual event: that the followers of Jesus sensed his
spirit among them, and that their subjective joy comprised a
kind of renewal of his life. The simple truth is that the
Resurrection is inseparable from the Incarnation itself; it is an
affirmation of the nature of the creation. God does not work
by magic, but in the laws of the very matter he has himself
exploded into existence and for a while holds in an expanding
balance – the universe. To be known about he must either be
discovered in the created order itself, by the use of human
reason, or he must be evident to our understanding in the only
way which is not incompatible with those same laws of
creation: by becoming one of us. Both means of knowing God
are available to us. In every culture on the planet men and
women have perceived the evidences of a Creator, and have
employed their capacity of reason to put their sense that this
is so into formal images of God, sometimes, alas, in grotesque
ways. God, for his part, entered the immediate experience of
humanity by taking upon himself the shared life of his
creatures: a supreme act of revelation which confirmed the
preceding intimations of his presence and also directly

179

opened the way of personal salvation to those whose response recognized and acted on his mercy.

It is essential to this divine initiative that God really was a man, and not either the mere *appearance* of a man (as some early heresies taught), or an actual human whom God 'adopted' as his earthly representation (a notion which crops up periodically in each century). Jesus was truly God and truly man. And here is a great paradox; for this was not a 'miraculous' occurrence, except according to a very careful definition of the word – modern people tend to use the concept of the miraculous as a kind of synonym for magic. It was an occurrence which fully used the material nature of the creation, thereby confirming that all God had made was a dimension of his purpose. Now resurrection stories were attached to numerous local divinities in the cults and mysteries of the ancient world, and were a familiar part of the expectations of those seeking religious help. Such cultic myths were full of bizarre and extraordinary miracles performed by the resuscitated leader. The Resurrection of Christ showed none of these excesses. Instead he returned to the Father; his earthly body, being fully God as well as fully man, ascending (or translating) with the entire power of the author of all things. It was an event both spiritual and material, a unique occurrence which signalled to the children of God – to all people, that is to say – that human life had been endowed with the dignity and purpose of eternal value. Whatever the dreadful imperfections of humanity, the man who is God beckons each one of us to follow him.

Ninety One

———

The burden that is light

ΒΟCΒ

There are so many people who just cannot cope with life. It is not the great problems which afflict them – decisions about philosophical or ultimate matters of general meaning: it is the struggle to get through daily existence. Things which to some of us seem readily resolvable or which we can absorb as part of the normal attrition of social life become, for others, oppressive realities of survival. There is nothing wrong with them; they are victims, merely, of a sense of proportion and a scale of priorities which leave them defenceless against an increasingly congested and professionalized world. It is one of the least felicitous aspects of the modern obsession with crime that prisons are being filled up with people who are not recalcitrant criminals but people who simply cannot cope. It also seems that the more we come to depend upon technology – which was supposed to make life easier – the more complicated daily exchanges become. And the managerial changes and structures of accountability which are now a part of the work-place add to the enclosing sense of lost control over individual choice. Having avoided Fascist and Marxist versions of totalitarianism, or at least suffered them for only an interlude (as in the case of most of Europe), the people of the end of the twentieth century are becoming the creatures of the Regulation State – slaves of laws governing the minutest areas of personal behaviour passed in order to secure our welfare and social morality. But it is not in the greater dimensions like these that people most

———

181

find their inability to cope: it is in the commonplace and smaller things, minor encounters of the daily round.

The modern response to such situations is welfare collectivism – the setting up of 'support groups' for people who cannot cope, or attempts to legislate the problems out of existence. Yet men and women have found the obligations of society oppressive ever since society itself was first established. For the inability to manage our lives has always been a part of the human condition; the structures of modern society merely focus it in a particularly acute fashion. The solution, to the extent that there is one, is not to involve people in therapeutic hobbies, or whatever; for their inability to cope will then merely declare itself in these substitutes also. The solution lies in recognition of human frailty as a normal and unavoidable component of each of us. Jesus said, 'Come to me you who labour and are wearied, and I will give you rest'. He added, however, 'take my yoke upon you, and learn from me'. The solution, therefore, is to become like Christ, a man 'gentle and lowly in heart' – without pretension, a man of simplicity, whose yoke is easy and whose burden is light. So many problems which afflict us are not worth worrying about anyway, and too great an absorption in our own anxieties is a persistent and subtle form of worldliness. Christ liberates us by offering the example of a man who experienced the fullness of earthly afflictions, even death on a cross, in complete selflessness. How much less weighty are the burdens we are called upon to endure.

Ninety Two

A discipline for the soul

ᏻᏺᏻ

It is sometimes noticed, and correctly, that support for religion in traditional societies had an element of entertainment. People went to church because there were few alternative leisure opportunities, and they derived a measure of recreational satisfaction from the social association. The popularity of revivalist preaching is perhaps explained in part by its vivacity and drama. Particularly in rural areas the Sunday gathering in church provided an exchange of news and a means of becoming acquainted with a wider world. The point should not be laboured, however, principally because attendances at church were not enormous. At the end of the eighteenth century, for example, fewer than fifteen per cent of the population attended the services of the Established Church, and perhaps a nearly equal number resorted to dissenting chapels. Even the Victorian religious boom, which was largely confined to the middle class, did not dramatically alter these levels of support for formal religion. The new churches then built remained unfilled. They represented the enthusiasm of the moralists rather than any inclination of the working classes to attend. But the element of entertainment was always significant. In a society of limited mobility, few educational opportunities, and low social expectation, the local church was often the place which provided some measure of relief from the travails of the work-place or the family. That society has long been buried, and a television aerial covers its grave.

The trouble is that modern people still expect religion to provide a kind of entertainment. There has been a secularization of the emotions – which are now routinely indulged for reasons which are emancipated from human moral seriousness. Each evening, before the screen, people's emotions move rapidly through a succession of manipulations quite unlike anything experienced in human society before. Like an addictive drug, furthermore, men and women now expect the same levels of emotional satisfaction from real life – and, where they think about it, from religion. Christianity is actually about submission to demands made by God, a surrender to a Sovereign outside our needs. Modern people, however, expect religion, instead, to provide immediate emotional satisfaction. For them it is thought to be a beautiful experience, a sense of interior peace, an aesthetically elevating sensation, a warm encounter with others, a dimension of the universal praise of 'caring'. In each of these facets, and in others, religion today is subordinated to individual emotional gratification; far from representing a consciousness of the terrible majesty of God, religion is becoming a mere accompaniment to personal expectations of emotional reassurance. It is high-minded entertainment. People choose their version of religion according to its capacity to satisfy their needs: the idea that their needs require any kind of discipline does not appeal. Each of us should be reminded every day that God's will and our perception of our own needs do not necessarily coincide.

Ninety Three

A morality for all
seasons

೫೦೦೪

It is sometimes said that the private life and moral behaviour of
a man or woman has no relevance in judging their fitness for
public office. Yet it is difficult to see how such a view can be
held. The issue is one of integrity. A person who is unreliable in
one dimension of his life is likely to be so in others. It is notably
true of public figures that those who are very active in one area
of their conduct are likely to be in all of them – as evidenced,
particularly, in sexual behaviour. But the principal unreality
about maintaining what some see as a 'liberal' attitude to
fitness for office is the separation of 'private' from 'public'
moral conduct. We would regard a person who entertains racist
opinions as unsuited; why, then, should we think someone who
has an unconventional record in sexual relationships any
different? Both rest on social acceptability, and most people
still regard sexual promiscuity as an unsatisfactory basis for
reliability. But there is a sliding scale of acceptability. We would
apparently eliminate child-molesters from public office but not
serial adulterers. Why do we think the second acceptable
behaviour? That can only be a *moral* judgement. If moral
approval is to be attached to *any* species of conduct, as surely it
unavoidably must, then what kind of religious or philosophical
basis do we employ as our standard of judgement? Christians
are actually the first to recognize the fact of human moral
frailty, and that people of tried ethical goodness may nevertheless lapse at some stage or other into wrong behaviour. That

---

185

does not make them wrong people, or hypocrites: they are simply people who have human characteristics, including moral fallibility. They would be foolish indeed who rejected the value of an ethical standard on the grounds that it could not always be met.

So the wise course is probably to recognize two sorts of behaviour for those in public office. The first is described by those who believe in an unstructured code of personal behaviour, or who are arbitrary and selective in applying moral norms. Such people are likely to be unsuited to office in a polity which respects ethical consistency. The second comprises those who try to live a moral life but fail. There is a Christian view about such as these, and it encourages a realistic acceptance of human weakness and a reluctance to condemn the whole person through a failing in one part of their being. Most in public life, happily, are probably in this category. But why restrict the matter to *public* life? Each of us is caught up in a nexus of relationships, and people depend on our moral reliability. And for each of us, also, our behaviour in one dimension of our lives is likely to be replicated in all dimensions. It is one of the fearful characteristics of sin that we always see ourselves as an exception when we venture into sinfulness – as if the moral laws somehow do not apply in our personal situation. Be thankful that the Christian God really does love sinners.

Ninety Four

The teaching of Christ

ଞଔଔ

Thursday was Ascension Day. Christians remembered the glory of the Saviour's departure from the world in the form he had taken in life – by then his risen life. Christians also celebrated the unbroken continuity of Christ's presence in the world – in his Church. Modern people tend to think of 'the Church' as an institution possessed of buildings and clergy, perhaps existing for purposes of spiritual welfare, and judged valuable in public esteem by the extent to which it encourages good works and avoids too precise or demanding a definition of its doctrinal basis. The Church in reality, however, is the physical presence of the Saviour in the world. It is the everlasting company of those people who preserve the words of Jesus and reinterpret them for each place and generation; there is a sense in which what the Church teaches is actually the teaching of Christ himself – continuing to unfold just as if he was with us still in his bodily form. That may initially seem a trite observation, but the fact is that the teaching of the Church is in a constant state of reinterpretation, since human culture is forever changing. The problem is in determining core or essential truths which may be rendered unambiguously and are stable, and in identifying, in contrast, applications of those teachings in the shifting circumstances of developing human understanding. If the teaching of Christ had been static, fixed for all time in the images and intellectual modules of the Palestine of his day, there would be no need for a dynamic role of the Church: its duty would have been simply to proclaim an unchanged set of verbal formulae. But the teaching of Jesus was not static – it was delivered to an evolving cultural environment and requires perpetual restatement. The truths proclaimed by Christ also *develop*, so that, like the mustard seed, new dimensions become visible in each age and time. What we call Christianity is an accumulating body of permanent enrichment, very far removed, indeed, from the dreadful modern reductionism that would depict it as merely an agency for human welfare, a sentimentalized adjunct to the modern pursuit of happiness, a therapy for those who are disconsolate.

As the body of Christ in the world the Church plainly has a unique office – that is why it has, in traditional language, been called 'holy'. How fearful, then, is the obligation placed on Christians themselves to ensure that what they teach as Christianity really is the authentic message of the Lord! It is an undertaking of such solemnity that it requires immense preparation and personal spiritual formation. Christians today are not perhaps as attentive as they might be to the cultivation of a spiritual life which, to be true to Christ, must be inseparable from all others seeking his service in time and in eternity. We have a responsibility to the company of the unseen world which transcends our own quest for individual religious satisfaction. The glory of the Ascension, thank God, provides us with the guidance of a Saviour who is risen and ascended and yet with us still.

Ninety Five

The vocation of interpretation

ଝଠ୦ଓ

Not much is thought of a scholar who selects from his data only those ideas which already coincide with his existing beliefs, or of a scientist who does not bother to consult all available variants to the probabilities already yielded by experiment or calculation. Yet that is precisely what many are prepared to do when deciding about religious truth. They simply do not learn the appropriate methods of enquiry, or realize that it is necessary to re-enter the cultural attitudes of those who formulated the traditions of thought which we have inherited. In biblical terms that means a rediscovery of the use made of images – in the spiritual vocabulary of the prophets, in the teaching of Christ himself. When questioned about the Parable of the Sower, Jesus actually explained both why he taught in images and what the meaning of the particular story was. This method of instruction, which was common in the ancient world, and especially so in the rabbinic style employed by Christ, has the enormous advantage that through the choice of everyday uses and symbols, available to the understanding of everyone, a series of meanings can be communicated simultaneously, in several layers of interpretation. But to understand the teaching it is necessary to hold a number of shared cultural assumptions – and it is these that people today do not bother with. As in so much else in the modern world, if something is not immediately attainable it is not pursued.

Let the point be illustrated by the image of the *rock*, perhaps one of the most common in the Bible. God himself, indeed, is 'the rock of our salvation'. For a people wandering in the desert a rock provides shade and shelter; rocky outcrops store rainwater; caves and fissures are homes, and the resort of solitaries seeking spiritual advance; rocks are dependable building material, and rocky heights can be defended against an enemy. As an image of refuge and dependability, therefore, the rock recurs in the Bible and in the teaching of Jesus. The confession of Jesus as the Christ made by Peter was at Caesarea Philippi: a shrine to Pan and rustic pagan divinities – a huge rock-face carved with symbols of Hellenistic piety. The rock as safety prompted Jesus's story about the man who built his house upon the rock. But the image always carried layers of meaning. For the rock which provides a dwelling also provides a tomb. It is death as well as life; and everywhere there were graves and chambers cut into the rock, like the sepulchre of Christ himself. Peter was the rock, Cephas, on which the Saviour built his Church; he was also, as in the Parable of the Sower, the rock on which the seed fell which became dried up, and failed to germinate. Thus Peter denied Christ at the time of his trial. And there is the great hope for all of us. Our redemption occurs despite the frailties of our natures, if we try to love God and to be faithful to him at the time of trial. The rock of dependence is also the rock which can be barren: it is us. We shall not fully understand the meaning of our calling, however, if we do not bother to learn the spiritual tradition in which it comes to us.

Ninety Six

Wheat and tares

ഇരു

The presentation of crime as a form of entertainment is not new. The Victorians had a great appetite for 'penny dreadfuls', and the cosy detective novel has an established place in the reading of many people. Children are socialized by 'cops and robbers' games (now under different names) which offer instruction in simple ethical models of behaviour through the demonizing of wrongdoers. All these had an obviously fictionalized context, however, or when centred on real events they had no actual consequences in the administration of justice: they comprised moral exhortation, not attempts to produce direct or popular involvement with the treatment meted out to criminals. But in our own day people are being encouraged to participate in the processes which affect the fate of criminals. Slowly, there is public acceptance of the idea that victims or their relatives should have a voice in sentencing policy; the press sometimes offers opinions on prison 'tariffs'. Popular television programmes in which crime is monitored, and individuals caught on security cameras are held up for identification, are disguised as exercises in public service. In reality they are introductions to street justice – very little removed, in emotional effect, from the gladiatorial exhibitions of antiquity or the sensationalism of public executions. It is not crime as entertainment so much as criminals for entertainment; and it is not Christian.

The numbers of those thought of as criminals is increasing. This is not due to a moral breakdown or the collapse of family values, as moralists like to think, but is simply because the law is remorselessly extending the definition of crime. In the name of welfare and public decency the minutest details of conduct are being subject to criminalization – mothers who leave young children unattended, minor sexual irregularities, failure to comply with the escalating complexity of financial regulation, drug use, petty acts of violence, and so forth. Many instances of small-scale bad behaviour, which once would have been dealt with inside the family or a social group, are now coming within the competence of the state. More and more people are being convicted. We are living in a new puritanism, with society self-consciously dividing itself between the supposedly virtuous and the evil-doers. As a dreadful paradox, many seem to believe this a Christian state of affairs – Christianity understood in an ethicized sense. Yet Christianity recognizes the universality of sin, and the inherent corruption of us all. Apart from a few authentic psychopaths there are no true 'criminal types'; there are just inadequate people, unable to cope, self-seeking, careless of others, in need of forgiveness. When crime is presented as entertainment, criminals are automatically de-monized, and we are all then the losers, because a false definition of the nature of humanity itself achieves priority. Christianity recognizes the need for sanctions in the ordering of society precisely because this is a fallen creation. But it recognizes also the moral frailty of us all, and the essential ambiguity of our attempts at virtue.

Ninety Seven

Forgiveness

ℰℐℭℬ

People tend to write their own agenda – both personal and social – into the message of Jesus. Thus he is made to be one who confers significance upon the various needs of the individual, who promises fulfilment of a list of emotional requisites. In public terms, he becomes the champion of justice and world peace, and brings consolation to the sufferings of humanity. But the essential message of Jesus was actually a call for personal repentance. It was expressed, furthermore, with great urgency: life was not given to each of us to dispose of as we will, but is the occasion to respond to specific commands which God makes; and as life is finite, so the need to recognize that the calling is immediate. There is no time to waste. Men and women are not sufficient in themselves to procure their own amendment, and what is wrong with them is at the very centre of their being – it is not some accident of conditioning, or incidental wrong choice produced by defective social environment, or the injustices of human organization. In the very heart of people there is a flaw which somehow affects our every action; it defines us as creatures who are less than the Creator, and whose capacity for self-correction is limited. Humanity, by definition in fact, is faulty. That is very definitely not what the modern world wants to hear. For we have come to estimate mankind as the centre of all things, and the needs of people and their claims as sovereign. The greatest good modern people can imagine is human welfare, and our moral culture has been reduced to a welfare programme. Jesus, however, as he moved among the people and taught them of the love of

193

God, began by setting out an essential pre-condition for salvation: they must repent. They must, that is to say, confess that they are not, in their own strength, capable of lifting themselves out of the dreadful moral ambiguity and actual wrong-doing that describes normal human conduct. Yet modern people do not recognize such a description of themselves – they have a notably exalted view of their capacity for contriving change, both personal and social. The change produced in people who submit to the rule of Christ, furthermore, relates to their spiritual condition and is not a transformation of their humanity – which remains flawed. That is particularly hard for modern people to understand. For, as in everything else, they look for instant results, consumer spirituality, a religion which appears to work by making people morally better.

What those who repent become, however, is not transformed in human terms – but forgiven. It is quite unrealistic, and in defiance of the nature of reality as set up by the Creator, to expect a kind of magic reconstitution of the personality. Obedience to God signals a spiritual condition that has changed – it makes our merely human failings, which continue, even more seriously hazardous to our spiritual integrity, but it does not eradicate them. Having become people who are forgiven, in addition, we have the obligation to forgive others, as the Lord's Prayer commands. Spirituality involves the evolution of a universal network of forgiveness, our invisible communion of the blessed which is the very beginning of knowing how to love God.

Ninety Eight

Keeping the truth

ເວ⦿

One of the most significant changes that has occurred in religion in Western countries over the last couple of centuries has been the removal of social impulsions encouraging observance. In traditional society religion was a mark of communal identity and social loyalty; it did not have to 'appeal' to people individually since it represented the collective subscription of society generally to higher purposes for human life. The religion conveyed in this way did not have to satisfy emotional needs or cater to personal claims to significance or meaning. It was true in itself, and the organization of society was witness to its authority: the commands of God were the ethical basis of human association. One consequence was that conversion from one religion to another involved radical statements about the nature of the state – hence the truly heroic stances of those, in the early Church for example, who accepted a new religious allegiance. This whole vision of things has now disappeared within Christianity, though it is fast reviving in Islam. Modern people are accustomed to privatized religion, and see it as an unquestionable right to pick and choose among available systems, or not to bother at all. The long-term effects of the Romantic Movement in taste, furthermore, have simulta-neously added the notion that religious belief is emotionally enriching, and that individuals can judge religious faith by the degree to which it assists uplift and a sense of beauty or serenity. Religion as therapy was born out of the idea that belief brought personal benefits which had little to do with the traditional obligations of obeying God because his command-ments are true. To modern people religious belief has to be comforting, palliative, bearing the promise of individual healing, a consolation against the ills of existence. The Churches, alas, show every sign of having adopted this understanding of religion themselves. They speak in marketing terms, of the 'appeal' of faith, of the 'need' which people have, of the benefit of 'fulfilled' lives. The current confusion of aesthetics and spirituality assists this: virtually anything which promotes a 'higher' dimension to life, virtually any human accomplishment in the arts, is regarded as somehow an indication of human religiosity. Serious music and serious art are acclaimed as witnessing, even if anonymously, to a divine inspiration. Children in schools are encouraged to suppose that moral consciousness and 'caring' attitudes are the very quintessence of religious faith. Marketing religion for a market society may well prove disastrous for authentic religion, however. For the commands of God are not naturally appeal-ing, and the way of the Cross is hard and often extremely unpleasant. At the centre of Christianity is a structure of doctrine, not a beautiful sentiment. It is about the evil of humanity and the need for men and women to repent; about the mercy of God, who forgives those who call upon him by making real sacrifices of their worldly preferences. The truths of religion are not just picked up at random selection – they have to be learned and applied. And that is not a message which the modern world will want to hear.

Ninety Nine

———

Declaring Christ

ಐಿಂಂೞ

There is something of a problem about what to recommend when people ask what they should read in order to understand Christianity. It is not much help to set the great classic works of Christian spirituality before them, since these already assume a knowledge of the faith – and were committed to paper in order to deepen an existing understanding, or to redirect its emphases in various ways. The Scriptures, too, are not a resource for beginners. The Bible requires explanation while it is being read; it is not, as some in the Western Protestant tradition used to suppose, self-explanatory. The Bible known to Jesus, the Old Testament, while wholly true as an account of God's progressive revelation of himself to a nomadic people, is not a unity and parts of it (the historical books) are certainly barbarous. The Old Testament describes moral teaching appropriate to a people who were in transition – it is about the education by God of a nation who through earthly experiences discovered true principles of faith. The process was dialectical: the Jews reacted with the folk customs and the tribal taboos of the people around them to produce an even account of what God wills. It does not readily convey meaning to an aspirant to truth in Camden Town. The New Testament is not an account of the life of Christ or a systematic statement of his teaching. It was written to *prove* the truth of Christianity to those who already existed in a living tradition of believers, the Church. The doctrines of the New Testament have therefore to be interpreted and understood *within* the same living tradition; its truths are not self-evident to novices. Sermons are not a very satisfactory way of conveying Christian doctrine in the modern world, partly because so few hear them, but mostly because people today are not used to receiving teaching in that particular format. The kind of sermon that is most appreciated today anyway consists of moral exhortation, personal testimony, or social prescription: a pity, but it is the case. As a way of passing on information about Christianity the new electronic retrieval systems are effective only for what they are – you can only retrieve what has been put in – and the Churches are rightly making what use of them they can. But the information revolution will probably prove in the end to obscure as much knowledge as it displays: there is so much available data that everything becomes relative, and religion is just another listing.

The Churches have a serious obligation to address the need to provide clear modern statements of what the *doctrines* of Christianity are. A model to begin with, perhaps, is the *Catechism of the Catholic Church* published by Rome in 1994. Christianity has existed so far within the historical and ideological developments of Hellenistic and Roman culture. These are not going to last for ever, and the faith will survive into whatever succeeds their inevitable demise only if it is clearly and systematically restated and reinterpreted, by the living company of believers who have always been its trustees. Clarity and confidence are the watchwords. God came into the world and consecrated our understanding of him in the person of Christ. We are charged with making that presence available to those who follow us.

One Hundred

———

Thy will be done

ଃଠାରେ

Leaders of Christian opinion sometimes speak as if there is a kind of natural attraction to religion, and that all they have to do is somehow to present the Faith in an appropriate manner and people will return to church. In this view of things religion is envisaged as an assistance to individual lives – as a consoling therapy, a system of explanation to meet the needs of people anxious to discover meaning. For some, it is supposed, religious belief is a way of satisfying emotional needs, a warm human message which can be the anodyne for the pains of living in a society that has lost its traditional social cohesives. Turning to religion as a way of getting through daily life is not a new phenomenon: far from it – it is what primitive religious practice was all about, but we are supposed to have progressed beyond it. In the ancient world, and in medieval Christendom, peasant labourers had their special saints to whom they could look for help in ploughing the field or encouraging the crop; knights had chivalrous representations of the Virgin to protect them in battle. Their instincts, movingly human in their way, were misplaced then and they are misplaced now. Religion is not a prop to help survive the travails of existence, nor is it given to men and women as an adjunct to their self-esteem. Modern people have an extremely developed view of the supposed 'sanctity' of humanity: their inclination is to look to religion, if they look to it at all, as a confirmation of merely human qualities – it becomes an affair of 'caring' and welfare and recognizing rights which people are thought to possess in virtue of their humanity. The modern idea of religion is also essentially non-discriminatory. God is no longer regarded as exclusive to a closely defined set of doctrines, but is a general description of generalized human values. Recent demonstrations of popular grief – as after the Hillsborough tragedy, for example, or the death of Diana, Princess of Wales – have perfectly expressed the current notion of what religion is thought to be. People have then looked for a warm and caring consecration of their inability to cope with normal human sorrow; they labelled commemorative bunches of flowers with the agnostic tag 'Why?' The Churches have accepted all this sort of thing as a legitimate rendition of authentic religiosity, and sought ways of exploiting it for recruitment strategies. These have so far proved barren. For theirs has been a resort to the methods of the market and to emotional sensationalism; the market and emotion, however, can actually provide better ways of satisfying such human demands than the Churches can. Who wants to go to church and be encompassed by a modest gathering of the conventionally respectable pawing their way through service books of Byzantine complication?

The truth is that religion is not a nice and consoling message, but an indictment of the evil in men and women. Its beginning is a call to repentance, just as Christ summoned people from their formal pieties, and their family values, to deny the world and take up their cross. Christian allegiance is a hard way, unattractive to the natural inclinations of men and women; those who choose it are setting their face towards emotional deprivation, not emotional luxuriance. The Man of Sorrows invites us to a joy which is not in correspondence with earthly expectations.

One Hundred and One

The eternal hope

ঙ৵দ্ব

Jesus said, 'be of good cheer, I have overcome the world'. To a people who are wrapped up in anxieties about health, security, stable employment, a happy family life – and all the other requirements of our social state – his words must seem oblique. But the life of Christ is the supreme example to humanity that there are purposes in our existence which transcend our priorities, however pressing they seem to be. We choose to forget the greater ends, or to give up believing in them; as in the Parable of the Sower, the eternal purposes are choked by thistles. For a few there are genuine problems of intellectual scepticism about the reality of religious understanding, and they are joined by a growing number of those fellow-travellers of the partially educated who think they are 'thinking for themselves' when they adopt passing fashions of thought in popularized tableaux of agnosticism. Most people, however, ignore the wider issues of truth and error, and simply allow their lives to be taken over by commonplace anxieties and trite priorities. Among them are no dramatic rejections of religious truth, and no earnest pursuit of philosophical alternatives – just a drift into inconsequence, the postponement of decisions about ultimate belief, an easy acceptance of the surface reality of things without the discomfort of extended thought. It was probably always so in human society: 'Is it nothing to you, all you who pass by?' The eternal presses close to the perceptions of men and women, yet they are impervious to its presence, preferring, instead, absorption by the only too accessible cares of daily existence. Asked about the purpose of human life, most declare their shocking conviction that it is the pursuit of personal happiness. Creatures who were made to be like angels, and who are endowed with the priceless capacities of reason and reflection, behave like animals in a farmyard whose horizons are determined by the next meal.

And yet there is hope for everyone. The God who made us, and is the author of all things, actually loves us as we are. God knows exactly what we are like, and how grievously we waste the gifts he has given us, forever mistaking the lower for the higher. And still he loves us. This is the great hope at the centre of Christianity. God is not indifferent to our fate; he did not set up the world and then leave it, and us, unattended. He loves us, and is engaged in our destiny. That is to say: he loves sinners. To the virtuous and the formally good he sends the message that they have their reward – in earthly terms, and in a manner which society may esteem but which is as finite as our lives are. To sinners, on the other hand, he promises life whose qualities are so approximate to his purposes that they can be said to be eternal. All that sinners need to do to possess this eternal life is to confess their sins and to deliver themselves to God's mercy. That is the substance of Christian hope, and it was confirmed in the sacrifice of God himself, who walked the earth and taught his people the way of eternity. He said: 'Let not your heart be troubled, neither let it be afraid.'

One Hundred and Two

———

The true cost of virtue

ଚ୨ଔଷ

At the centre of the Christian life is service. God is served by us not only directly, through the offering of perpetual praise, but indirectly by serving one another. The one who is greatest in the kingdom of heaven is also the one who is most lowly in the world – who is, as Christ made himself, the servant of others. It is easily said and much less easily fulfilled, partly because the concept of service for its own sake is largely absent from modern consciousness. In our society the notion of *service* has been replaced by that of *caring*. They are not the same thing. 'Caring' is anyway rather a rhetorical device, employed as a synonym for moral probity in a highly selective fashion. Although children are exhorted in school, for example, to become 'caring' people, and to exhibit 'caring' natures, the actual content of what caring implies is rather vaguely rendered – and would seem to involve respecting the beliefs of others provided those beliefs may be considered politically correct. It would also seem to involve the performance of such good works as the individual could reasonably expect to receive in return. Caring is thus an exercise in calculated hedonism, derived from an unstated ideological position. If an enquirer should ask (though few in practice do) of what theoretical or ideological system these caring acts are an application, he would not receive a coherent answer. For there is not one. To identify a basis in religious morality, for example, would offend against that dogma of political correctness which contends that all religious positions are of equal validity; to argue for a basis in traditional cultural inheritance would likewise encounter the claim that all cultures are to be venerated. The modern concept of caring in fact derives from the secular elevation of humanity; it is an undefined humanism, and is an almost perfect expression of the materialists' conviction that people are to be respected for their humanity rather than because of any rules derived from their transcendence. The equivalent disposition in the ancient world was 'common decency', and was regarded then as the lowest level of human responsibility, without which a man was a barbarian. Our predecessors would have been astounded that such a minimal practice of human decency should, after a couple of thousand years, be taught to children as the highest good.

Christian service, in contrast, is the application of a theology. People are to be served because they are God's children, and not out of supposedly enlightened self-interest. Christian service is the enactment of belief in higher purposes for human life, and it is due to God before it is due to ourselves. At its heart is self-denial, in order that the practitioner should recognize a personal culture which belongs to God – the very ownership of the personality by God. Service is for its own sake, but it is not an end in itself. It is sacrificial, for it denies the priority of personal need in order that the Christ conveyed in others may be served.

Taking up the Cross

🕮

The notion that religious belief has to 'appeal' to people, and that its essential basis is in emotional need rather than in obligations owed to a divine being, was given an enormous stimulus by the progressive withdrawal of governmental and social support for religion over the past two centuries. The political order no longer sees itself legitimized by the sanction of religion, and it is less and less inclined to consider the promotion of religious belief among the citizens as part of its duties. Public debate about the place of religion in state schools, for example, is all about fostering decency and moral behaviour, and about recognizing the cultural inheritance rather than the doctrines of Christianity. Family ties are no longer regarded in terms of shared religious identity, and so the most basic unit of society has secularized itself. Family prayers – always, anyway, a feature of bourgeois society, rather than society in general (but that is actually true of most of the characteristics of what are sometimes called 'family values') – have disappeared. To 'appeal' to people religion has become represented as something which is by its nature *nice*: consoling, emotionally satisfying, perhaps aesthetically gratifying, imparting significance to the existence of the individual. The Churches have themselves now come to accept this definition, and unthinkingly proclaim evangelistic strategies which assume that religious belief will add to the happiness of the individual. Saving people, in past essays of evangelism, informed them, in contrast, about their depravity and the fate that awaited the unregenerate soul. The Churches' adoption of the notion of religion in terms of appeal indicates the extent to which they have adopted the secular agenda in general, including its supposition that human life is centred in the pursuit of happiness. Christianity has gradually been unconsciously redefined as an adjunct to human pleasure rather than a set of obligations owed to God. That is how it is now presented to the public by its leaders, and that is what the public expect to hear. The message is about what religion can do for them, and not about what they can do for God. But the numbers who respond even to the redefined version of Christianity are increasingly modest; the secular alternatives are better in the same competition. Reduced to an affair of caring about human need – which is the conclusion to be drawn from listening to the average sermon – Christianity emerges as a dimension of ordinary humanism, and scarcely seems necessary.

In fact Christianity is not, as all authentic religion is not, nice. It does not exist to bolster the modern emphasis on the priority of human needs: it suggests, instead, that men and women are deeply corrupted and stand in need of forgiveness; and it proclaims that, despite appearances of human improvement in some particulars, mankind will be forever suffused by sin. An understanding of Christianity founded on emotional satisfaction will be false: Christianity rests on the objective existence of a God who makes real demands which, built into individual lives, imply privation and personal surrender of choice. The representation of worship in aesthetically satisfying forms is a human by-product: the purpose of worship is the honouring of God. We offer the best that moves our emotions in the hope that it will prove pleasing to God, and in the process we unavoidably move ourselves. But worship does not exist for what it does for us, and it is definitely not, as modern people suppose, a kind of therapy or a demonstration of human camaraderie.

One Hundred and Four

Dust to dust

ॐ

Religious belief has always been associated with the super-natural, and it cannot be doubted that some today turn to Christianity in anticipation of an experience of supernatural forces. There is a worryingly pervasive fascination with the idea of paranormal phenomena in modern society, as evidenced by the popularity of television series on these themes. People who would be ashamed to believe in magic in normal circumstances appear to revel in it when it is presented as science fiction. The clergy will confirm that many who consult them are primarily interested in the supernatural dimension of what they think of as Christianity. The miraculous events described in the Bible, and the miracles attributed to Christ himself, seem to testify to the authenticity of supernatural powers within religion; ecclesiastical miracles have been recorded evenly across the history of the Churches. Many believe they can communicate with the dead, and even more look to prayer as a means of actually rearranging reality in order to achieve desired ends. But God has called men and women to work with him in the progressive development of the creation, and has endowed them with the faculties of reason and reflection to enable them to do so. Prominent in their consequent discoveries are accounts of earthly phenomena which increasingly exclude the likelihood of supernatural forces determining actual events.

The universe which God created is 'natural', and so, therefore, is our world and all its phenomena – including us. Everything operates according to laws and probabilities which may ultimately be known, or at least conjectured, since the

207

creation is 'real' and not an illusion. There is no need for 'supernatural' explanation: God has revealed his purposes – whose grand design we cannot know – in the creation, and it is our only source of knowledge. There are no mysterious intimations or visions which do not derive from our own material constitution. The philosophical materialists are right to the extent that they explain how matter has determined our perception of ourselves and of the world; they are wrong in supposing that this 'natural' order is without design or purpose. Christians believe that the universe expresses a will, and accept with humility the otherwise galling fact that humans cannot know *all* that is willed by the Creator. Science is showing that the universe is a less predictable place than had previously been supposed, and that the laws of matter (if it is still possible to use such a phrase) involve more apparently arbitrary aspects than mechanistic thought had allowed. But, taken all in all, reality must now be seen as a 'natural' series of phenomena. Christians believe that the Creator, in wishing to make himself known to his creatures, became himself, at an historical moment, a part of the creation. Christ stood outside of the created order and yet was of its substance: this is the central truth and the cardinal paradox of the Christian religion. We are invited, as natural beings in a world that operates naturally, to follow his teaching and to love the things which he loved. We are also required, as persons of reason and reflection, to emancipate the divine from the merely human in the circumstances of his life on earth, and to recognize in Jesus a person who, alone, transcended material reality in a great revelation of the divine love.

One Hundred and Five

———

Raised to glory

ಎಂಜ

The Feast of the Ascension, celebrated last week, should not be marginalized, or explained in symbolic language, as modern Church leaders are inclined to do. For it marks a decisive moment in the purpose of the Incarnation itself, and is inseparable from the Resurrection. If Christ really did rise from the grave his departure from the world must have been equally miraculous – equally at variance with previous experience. Legends have always persisted that he remained alive, and some have sought to identify his tomb: an indication of credulity rather than authenticity. For Christians the proof of the Resurrection and the Ascension, and the confirmation of the promises made to his followers by the risen Christ, is the existence of the Church itself – his body in the world. The life of Jesus, and the fact of his Resurrection, plainly involved 'miraculous' events, and it is not possible to accept the claims of Christianity without acknowledging them. But when God himself, the Creator of all things, was in the world and sharing in its very substance, the laws which ordinarily describe the acts of humans were not applicable. The works of healing performed by Christ were within the expectations of those who followed him; they were intended, like the Incarnation itself, to make the heavenly knowable in human terms – in terms of what humans expected of religious phenomena. They were done with a certain reserve, a kind of concession to human understanding; Jesus himself wearied of the popular desire for 'a sign' or for 'wonders', but recognized that they were part of the spiritual culture of the ancient world.

The central events of the life of Christ – the Virgin Birth, the descent of the dove at his Baptism, the Resurrection and the Ascension – were of a different nature, however. These were not folk miracles, given in order to convey or signify religious authority in the manner expected by those who heard Jesus, and therefore comparable to those supposedly performed by many spiritual leaders as evidence of their chrism. The central miracle of the Incarnation itself and its consequences were unique. When God was in the world as a person the distinction between the 'supernatural' and the 'natural' disappeared, for the Creator of all things was, as it were, creating as he went along: yet he was fully a man – a man using the expectations of his day to convey his message and authority. This was a long way from the notion, so widespread today, as in the past, that all religious experience involves an acquaintance with the 'supernatural', and that reality today can be changed by religious faith. The most perfect form of prayer given by Jesus to his followers was devoid of petitions for miraculous cures or personal exemptions from physical hazards – the substance of so many prayers offered by modern people. We live in a real creation, not a magic side-show; in the world God is known about through the natural order. He is also and supremely known in Christ, the great focus of revealed truth. God's presence in Christ was, in our terms, 'miraculous'. Our lives, in contrast, are 'natural', and the world we inhabit operates wholly through the material order established by God.

One Hundred and Six

How to know God

ಬ೦೦ಶ

In the ancient Jewish understanding of things God operated through a particular culture and national experience to reveal his nature. Truth cannot be known if it is rendered in terms which are too generalized: it needs particular expressions and embodiments. In Christianity, which is rooted in the Jewish spiritual tradition, God revealed himself by becoming a man – the supreme example of universal truth assuming a particular form in order to be known. Modern people, in contrast, are sceptical of localized renditions of truth and prefer the general. They claim, for example, a love of humanity. But no one can love humanity, because it is too various and too ambiguous; it is only possible to love individual humans. Preference for the general over the particular suits a people like us, who are wary of ideology and think it is mature to be pragmatic. Mass education, the information explosion, the virtues supposedly annexed to democratic practice, have encouraged modern people to imagine they are 'thinking for themselves' when they decide about what they are to believe. In reality, as it happens, these very conditions have only provided an extremely effective means of mass manipulation of opinion, and the numbers of those who genuinely 'think for themselves' are doubtless as small as they have always been in proportion to the population as a whole. The pervasive sense that mature people will be impatient of precise definitions of truth is, however, only applied in relation to religion and the philosophic bases of public policy. People today are very precise, and insist on very minute definitions, about the agenda of 'political correctness', or what constitutes social behaviour, or human rights.

The Church has a problem with all this, even though it usually chooses not to address it directly. Christian truth is the truth revealed in Christ – who did not ruminate in imprecise terms about spiritual beauty or the loveliness of mankind, but delivered a stark rebuke to a generation which was neglecting the laws of God. Christ was the universal in the particular form of a man. It is difficult to imagine a more precise way of conveying exact truths, and Christianity, accordingly, is a religion which requires exclusive allegiance from its adherents. Modern people like to suppose that there is 'truth in all religions', and that men and women should, in effect, adopt the religion suited either to their personal needs or to their encompassing culture. They are largely ignorant of the doctrines of Christianity, and take them to be all about mere human decency; this hugely assists the process of relativizing the religion. Christianity is also undermined by the simultaneous assault upon its historical authority made by emphasizing what is perceived as a record of persecuting others and encouraging warfare – choosing to ignore the comparable records of all other religions, and of all peoples at all times. Among the things Christianity is precise about is the sinful state of men and women, including those who seek to serve Christ despite the inherent corruptions of their nature. All religions are *not* of equal value, nor are they simply localized variations of a universal truth. In Christianity the people of the world are offered individual salvation, and that is a very particular and a very precise gift.

One Hundred and Seven

The mercy of God

ೞ‍ೲ

The marvel of Christianity is the great love of God: that he bothers with humanity at all. It is easier to believe in a God whose power created the universe and appointed life than it is, on the evidence of the state of humanity itself, to believe that he involves himself with the work of his hands. Despite the modern inclination to exalt humans, and to mistake their technical capabilities for virtue, the record of the centuries, of all cultures and all peoples, shows that men and women are inherently corrupted. That, too, is the biblical account of them. Nothing we can achieve merits salvation, and the good that we would do – as St Paul remarked – we do not do. By most of the standards that might be proposed to judge success, humanity fails. It was once pointed out by Jonas Mekas, the American underground film director, that the lack of critical acclaim for Louis Malle's *Zazie dans le Métro* was not surprising. God, he said, had created failures too: witness mankind. The cosmic scheme implicit in deism, and perhaps in modern agnosticism, at times seems appealing; that God set up the world and then left it to operate according to the laws of creation and did not interfere with its course or with the fate of its creatures. In Christianity, however, there is a firm belief that the world does indeed proceed according to the laws of creation, and that meaning is conveyed to men and women through material reality, and not by some kind of magic, but that God also made himself known directly. Humanity was lifted from the rest of created things, and endowed with the gifts of reason and reflection; and then, astonishingly, was called by God to share with him in the development of the planet. But the nature of men and women was not changed. They remained, and always will be, flawed, bearing the image of God yet distorted by the fact of being so much less than God. Their highest attempts at godlike understanding are frustrated by their condition, and their most noble essays in altruism are ambiguous. The record of human life through the centuries says it all; and the twentieth century, when mankind is supposed to have achieved enlightenment, has been, in those terms, the most dismal of all. Mass education has not elevated moral consciousness. The two most horrific wars in history, both in scale and in the levels of atrocity, originated in the most educated and most civilized of the continents.

Men and women are not changed by the practice of religion, either. In a number of particulars they may acquire more effective and disciplined living through the adoption of rules – a feature also of many secular organizations like political youth movements. But Christianity does not change human nature: it consecrates individual sinners for Christ's service. A quick glance down the pews will confirm that human corruption is not eliminated in those who turn to God: it is, however, forgiven. This is the great measure of God's love, and the hope of everyone. Christianity is not a mere ethicist system, concerned primarily with good behaviour – it is addressed to those who find they *cannot* behave well. It is the company of the forgiven. The most despised child-molester, violent criminal, cruel racist, may rank higher than the most formally virtuous in the kingdom of heaven. For Jesus calls sinners, not the righteous, and those who try to follow him, despite the dreadful facts of their weakness, are those to whom he gives the crown of glory.

One Hundred and Eight

Not having everything

ℰℐℂℬ

Self-denial is not very greatly recognized or practised as a virtue in our society. Indeed, it is scarcely recognized at all – except, perhaps, to the extent that certain habits or the consumption of certain foods, for example, may impair health. The reason for self-denial, in such cases, is plainly self-interest and relates to material well-being. Occasionally self-denial is conceded as a necessary condition for securing the liberties of others, and then, again, it is self-interest which promotes acceptance. The young are exhorted to save instead of spending on credit to obtain desired goods, and here, once again, the intention is not really moral or spiritual formation: it is to spare them the pain of subsequent debt – the motive is practical. The lives of so many today are passed in a gentle self-indulgence which would have shocked our predecessors, and which stands, incidentally, in dreadful contrast to the unavoidable privations of existence in large parts of the developing world. Our culture now contains nothing which suggests that self-denial may be virtuous for its own sake, and the religious teaching which once considered it an important aspect of the spiritual life has largely been abandoned – even amongst those who still adhere to Christianity. We regard ourselves as entitled to the good life; whatever may be deemed an enhancement of that – provided it has no material disadvantages – is judged a kind of birthright. Rights, in fact, have a lot to do with it: the moral culture of rights, with the catalogue of human rights at its centre, is hardly likely to honour personal privation, even when voluntarily entered into.

Life itself, however it is arranged by social need or political contrivance, is about *not* having what we want. Most would probably say that their priority is happiness: freedom from illness, stable and secure relationships, personal comfort, emotional satisfaction, and so forth – the very areas where self-indulgence may so easily be practised with scarcely any consciousness that moral harm is being done to the individual. For these are also the areas which feed upon themselves, where expectations are forever extending, and where satisfaction proves illusory. To seek self-discipline in the small aspects of personal living is to cultivate moral and spiritual awareness of the need for the same quality in larger matters; self-denial becomes the essential precursor of enlightenment. It is almost impossible to declare this in a society which denies itself nothing. But Christianity has always recognized it. Jesus told his followers to take up their cross; truth was achieved not by the easy declamation of general principles but by arranging individual lives so that the manner in which a person lives assists spiritual understanding. The world is a place where lessons are to be learned; it is not an interlude of hedonism before everlasting bliss. What we become through the accumulation of spirituality here is what endures for eternity.

One Hundred and Nine

_____

More than human need

ಋಁೞ

This summer a sizeable group of Christian activists toured several middle-eastern countries begging the Islamic inhabitants to forgive them for the Crusades. And it is evidently not only modern Christian believers who find the notion of warfare on behalf of religious truth offensive; so do very many among the Western intelligentsia, and it is now held, indeed, that religion itself has been discredited by its association with violence – and not only in the distant past, like the Crusades, but in Northern Ireland or the Balkans. People who really *do* believe in their values, however, defend them at high cost. The NATO war in Kosovo is a case in point. This was trumpeted by its advocates as 'the first moral war in history', fought not out of any national self-interest but in the name of humanity. It was Ethical Foreign Policy in practice. In reality, of course, it was just another example of a war waged for religion – for the tenets of the secular religion of Humanity. The war in Kosovo fits perfectly into the long list of religious wars as soon as it is recognized that the modern veneration of human life has in effect succeeded Christianity as the moral basis of Western society.

It is actually very important to realize this. For Christians themselves are among the first to absorb the religion of Humanity without any clear consciousness that what they are about is the secularization of their own religious beliefs. God is being replaced by man and his needs as the first priority. Life itself is becoming more important than what individuals exist to believe. Religion is being relegated to the realm of mere emotional satisfaction and therapeutic support, or is understood as a set of ethical principles. It is human need which now occupies the centre of public consciousness of a 'higher' purpose. Whereas religion is judged divisive and full of seemingly archaic precision ('dogma'), concern for human life, which everyone can agree about, unites men and women from different societies and projects achievable goals in the general ideals of justice and peace. How easily this is all made to correspond to basic Christianity! Once all the precise commands of God about the requirement of individual repentance, and all the obligation of worship, have been syphoned off, the residue of ethicism can so readily be equated with the Christian love of neighbour. But there is a problem: Jesus did *not* say that human life was sacred, the way we do; he did *not* declare human need as the essential spring of moral action; and he was *not* indiscriminate about the Divine – very much not. If we would be followers of Christ we must give up placing ourselves and our own estimate of our entitlements at the heart of human life, and recognize, instead, that what Jesus spoke about was our moral frailty and our personal corruption. The whole point about the divine redemption of humanity was that humanity did not deserve it. The miracle of God's love is that he cares for us *despite* ourselves. The beginning of religious wisdom is the consciousness of human sin. Instead, we set too high an estimate on our own lives. Jesus was not a human rights activist but a Saviour; he did not come to inform us that our lives were sacred, but that we need forgiveness.

One Hundred and Ten

_____

A diminished state

❧

Ours is conventionally represented as a tolerant society – or, at least, one that is more tolerant than in the past. And religion, indeed, is often blamed for causing intolerance, both in the past and in those places today where conflict exhibits religious difference. But this is not a more tolerant society; it is merely one that has shifted the things it is intolerant about. A list of politically correct dogmas will show at once that modern intolerance has moved from the heavenly to the earthly – we do not pass laws to criminalize wrong beliefs about God, as our predecessors did, and as our contemporaries among Islamic or Hindu revivalism do. Instead we legislate against unacceptable views about humanity: our laws criminalize disapproved attitudes in matters of race, for example, or sexuality or parenting. We speak, amusedly, about the 'nanny state', in partial recognition of the increasing entry of public regulation into areas of conduct which were once thought best left to individual initiative. We fail to notice that the type of issues being brought into public regulation are actually very materialistic – they are about human welfare. Until very recent times civilized societies used the authority of the state to promote and to protect 'higher' ideals: the nature of the divine, the ultimate purpose of social existence, and of life itself. Society was seen as aspiring upwards towards realities which were sometimes only to be attained in eternity. The decay of religious belief in the West, and the notion that the secular, plural society is a mature society, have despatched all that. But what we have not noticed is that what has arrived in place of the old confessional state – anonymously, because without a coherent philosophical basis or available label – is a society which aspires *downwards*. All the old higher ideals have become controversial because not universally approved, so what is left is the common denominator of material self-interest. The state now, in effect, sees its 'higher' purpose in the service of human material needs. This is disguised in the intense moralism of public rhetoric, for the concern with human material welfare is represented as enlightened ethicism. It is the culture of the 'caring society'. There is a curious hint here that among inherent human attributes is a kind of pathological moralism. Having de-throned God, and elevated human need in his place, men and women seem to be incapable of not enforcing their convictions on everyone else. They get away with it for a number of reasons. In the first place the laws which are passed to enshrine the new enthusiasm for humanity are often in themselves laudable. Secondly, the leaders of religion are keen to support the emerging secular theocracy of the religion of Humanity: is not human welfare a part of the Christian message? And thirdly, there is now no disposition amongst the intelligentsia and public figures to support state promotion of non-materialist higher ideals – especially since the prevailing humanism, despite its patent materialism, is paradoxically acclaimed as itself constituting a 'higher' dimension. The intolerance of our day will not countenance those who dare to harbour heretical reservations about the virtues of humanity.

One Hundred and Eleven

Remembrance

࿔

What exactly is being remembered on Remembrance Sunday? It is certainly lost lives, but is it also in some sense a commemoration of the causes for which people died? This would often seem to be implied when the lives sacrificed in the Second World War are linked with the triumph of democracy or the defeat of Nazism. But the custom today is to use Remembrance Sunday as the occasion to remember *all* the war dead, on all the various sides of what was a series of multiple conflicts – of Japanese as well as of Americans in the Pacific, of Germans as well as French or Russian or British in Europe. And that is surely the right thing to do. Most of those who died in the wars of this century have been conscripts. Theirs was involuntary sacrifice for they had no control over their destiny and were not consulted, even in democratic countries, about the justice of the causes for which they eventually died. In many ways this makes their heroism even more admirable, and the tragedy of their slaughter all the more to be marked by national recognition. For the moral value of an act is not diminished because the morality is compulsory: law does not cease to be moral because we are obliged to obey it. Genuinely free agency is a very rare commodity indeed in human life, since so much of what we do is determined by conditions over which we have no choice, and even apparently self-conscious choice is in reality filtered by the false consciousness inseparable from all personal formation. Those who die in warfare are serving on our behalf, as agents of the state, in furtherance of ideals or policies which some may, and some may not, believe in. Their sacrifice is the nobler for being made without ideological preconditions.

Remembrance is most valuable, therefore, when it centres on the individual, on the actual soldier or sailor or airman, who lived and breathed and belonged to a family and loved a home and had hopes of better things. It is an occasion to recall particular people over the long passage of the years, so that they will briefly be alive again in our memory – or, as in the case of younger generations, in the imaginings of those who have been told about them. Every child who has had no possibility of personal acquaintance with one of the war dead might be encouraged to 'adopt' a name from a local war memorial, and commend its owner to the mercy of God and the everlasting gratitude of those who survive. For Remembrance is also a time to remind ourselves that the wrath of men and women is not God's way, and that human society, however organized and whatever good or evil may attach to its actions, stands under God's judgement and needs his forgiveness. That is why Remembrance is devalued if it becomes a mere adjunct of 'civic religion', as it so easily does in Britain. Then it loses its vital function of recalling the memory of the real people who are its purpose. The dead can only live again, in earthly terms, if we allow them to be present in our thoughts.

One Hundred and Twelve

———

Family values

ೞഔ

Christian sanction is now conventionally given to the main-tenance of the family as an essential condition for a properly constituted society. This is reasonable enough, especially since there really is no alternative: people either live together in voluntary units with their own primary loyalties – which is what family life is – or they are organized by external bodies, probably institutions of the state in a collectivist polity like ours. The latter has been tried on many occasions in history and is plainly inapplicable in our circumstances. The current volatility of family units, however, is not a pointer to the breakup of family life as such, as so many seem to think, but only to the fact that some individuals reassemble family groups less formally than has been considered either desirable or moral in the past of the culture. One-parent families, serial relationships, and same-sex liaisons are not actually destructive of the idea of the family: they reconstitute it on a different basis and without certain legal constraints and guarantees. Only a very few really experiment with communal living, and those who do quickly become categorized as weird, 'hippy' survivors of 'sixties' liberation, self-sufficiency freaks, enemies of decency. So when the Churches identify conventional family life as a Christian model they are still talking about a norm. But what do they mean?

The 'family' used in the present eulogy of 'family values' – which is projected as the guardian of moral order and the essential means of raising children in stable conditions – is a very recent concept. It is also a class concept. The family, in

223

this sense, describes the aspirations and social practices of the Western bourgeoisie in the period between about 1880 and about 1960. This was when children were endowed with a romantic innocence quite at variance with observable reality; when 'respectability' withdrew the young from the socializing of the streets which their working-class contemporaries still received; when marriage ceased to be a social arrangement, and when the intended partners raised expectations of romantic love and shared interests; when middle-class families retreated behind net curtains and family life privatized itself. What we call 'the family' today is actually an enormously complicated phenomenon, but its broad characteristic is the assumption that family members will experience the increasingly diverse choices offered by modern culture as a unit. This, as it happens, is clearly difficult to achieve. People are now too individualized to be content with life in the hothouse of the idealized family unit: mass education, heightened expectations to varied experience, the application of consumer instincts to the acquisition of values and lifestyles themselves, sexual freedom, and early maturation of children, cultural diversity, and numerous other considerations, are progressively dismantling the bourgeois ideal of the family at a rate which is alarming the moralists. But they need not take fright. Humans are extraordinarily adaptable, and they are already rearranging themselves in perfectly viable alternative modes. Christians in Africa, with the approval of the Lambeth Conference, have acclaimed polygamy as an acceptable lifestyle. Adjustment to received notions of the family in Britain, after that, seems quite mild.

One Hundred and Thirteen

Accepting ourselves

୫⃝ଔ

Sinfulness is something we tend to ascribe to others and not to ourselves: it is the oldest human failing. In the modern world, to make it worse, we think in collective terms – mass education, the emergence of the collectivist state, the multiplicity of information supplied by television, all encourage us to see evil in collective terms too. For us 'sin' is a matter of wrong ideology, or vicious opinions about race, or religious bigotry, or social prejudice: rarely do we acknowledge the evil in ourselves. Yet the larger evils derive from us each as individuals, and it is in us that the seat of corruption lies. We do not see it; the idea of a fallen world is not part of modern culture. Men and women are regarded as basically good, as possessed of numerous rights which extend so far as the right to a fulfilled and happy existence, and as endowed with considerable personal significance which others ought to respect. This last, which we take so much for granted, and which we elevate to the level of the 'sacred' when we speak of the 'sanctity of human life', is a relatively recent concept. For most of human history people were thought of as rather miserable creatures, inherently corrupt, and given to wickedness. They needed the sanction of authority if social order was to be maintained. Modern people, in contrast, are virtually incapable of appreciating self-discipline; ours is a culture of self-indulgence – and especially of the indulgence of the emotions. People in traditional society knew that human sinfulness was such that without disciplined living there would be moral chaos. And so it is proving to be. Discoveries about the nature of the creation are tending to confirm the ancient belief in the insignificance of humanity – an excrescence on the surface of a speck of space debris – just at a time when modern ideology is insisting increasingly on the sovereign importance of human life. Christianity, however, has always emphasized the worthlessness of men and women in cosmic terms; and it has also always insisted on their value to God who is their Creator, and who also, in an astounding act of grace, has revealed himself, and through a supreme sacrifice has offered them redemption. Human life therefore discloses the dignity of those who are called to transcendence. But human life, nonetheless, is borne by individuals who remain inherently sinful and are, in relation to the Creator, without rights.

What modern society needs is instruction about personal sin. There is plenty of declamation about the large errors of racism, sexism, ecological irresponsibility, and all the rest of it – necessary, doubtless, but nonetheless in practice distracting attention from the priority which should be placed on the individual sinfulness of each of us. Human life is not sacred, and we are not sacred. We are, however, the wretched bearers of an extraordinary gift: the promise which Christ holds out to those who acknowledge their corruption and ask for his forgiveness. It is such a simple thing. And if we accept the responsibility of our own sinfulness we shall be much better able to cope with the collective sinfulness of human action in the world.

One Hundred and Fourteen

———

The mote and the beam

ℰ✺ℭ

It is common for friends or relatives of someone accused of a fearful crime to say that they know them well and that they are utterly incapable of the evils attributed to them. There is an understandable and wistful humanity in this; but it is unrealistic. All of us are capable of just about anything, given the appropriate circumstances. It is widely acknowledged that in a general breakdown of order – in some apocalyptic vision of a nuclear war, for example – people would fend for themselves with little regard for traditional moral constraint. Yet the conditions for such a suspension of moral regularity occur in individual lives, in less dramatic form, all the time. It may well be a matter of chance and opportunity, as much as of moral fortitude and personal nobility of character, whether or not the actions which result offend law and convention. Here is another example of the universality of sin. Humanity is by definition corrupted, and even in the lives of the most worthy and esteemed people the potential horrors of our fallen natures are all present. Who is virtuous in a visible set of acts may well be vicious in hidden or less noteworthy dimensions of life. This is a phenomenon of humanity which should temper the inclination, which is alive now as ever it was, to demonize criminals. People who murder, or commit dreadful sexual offences, or perpetrate atrocities in situations of conflict, or whatever, are not a separate species of being. They are most likely to be just like us; their lives, however, at some moment inexorably caught up in situations where ordinary human weakness escapes restraint. Only a very few would seem to be

227

truly pathological criminals; most convicted of crime in our society are normal human beings whose lives have placed them where circumstance betrays morality. There are more criminals than in the past not because of some great moral collapse in society but because the law is, in our day, being extended into increasingly more precise details of daily living, and so criminalizing actions which once were regarded as acceptable if regrettable. It is the goal-posts of the public sense of proper behaviour which are changing. A bloody affray outside a pub, which thirty years ago would have broken up without further action, today results in custodial sentences. In a sanctimonious society of moralists like ours the demonizing of others is always a popular option.

Christians, however, are taught to love their neighbour as themselves, and that includes the rapist, the child-molester, and the racist. Their sins are no worse than many that all of us commit all the time in acts of cruelty and vindictiveness, of jealousy and envy – acts which are not punishable in the courts. But they are acts which are as deeply corrosive to the ideals of an ordered society as if they were. Hidden from public view, and unremarkable because of their awful frequency, the daily sinfulness of men and women, of all of us, is what actually describes human life. What we need is forgiveness, not punishment of others; and that is precisely what the religion of Jesus offers.

A clear message

৪১০৪

Although it is true that Christians today have a great capacity for identifying the political and moral passions of the moment as essential embodiments of religious teaching, it is also true that very many outside the Church approve of their doing so. Knowledge of Christian doctrine is slight. This is not to refer to hostile observers but to nominal Christians, or to those who assess the faith simply as part of received Western culture. It is surprising – and a shocking commentary on the way religious education is sometimes conducted in schools – to discover how little even members of the intelligentsia seem to know about the real nature of Christianity. The Churches themselves must bear a lot of the blame: they are plainly poor propagandists for doctrine, having become more enthusiastic about worldly applications. It is this priority of the Church leaders, the ethical dimensions of the Faith, which encourages the widespread tendency in society to regard Christianity as a kind of benign handmaid of the prevalent humanism, a sanctifying of whatever solutions to human ills agitate the heated consciences of the high-minded. No one seems to want to know about doctrine: about the demands and sacrifices which authentic religion imposes, about the exclusivity of God, and the imminence of judgement.

When they are not redefining religion as a mere affair of social concern and enthusiasm for humanity people seem to regard it as having value (if it is deemed to have value at all) in reinforcing self-esteem. Their lives are of such importance, they imagine, that they are owed an enormous range of benefits –

including ultimate explanations about the purpose of life itself, and certainly embracing personal emotional satisfaction. Christianity is in this sense reinterpreted as a beautiful idea: Jesus is made to consecrate an extensive assemblage of individual demands for a fulfilled and meaningful existence. In practice people put together their own understanding of the Christian faith, based on priorities of their own choosing, quite uninhibitedly adding favoured bits of other beliefs. The only unifying element appears to be pleasure; religion is conceived to be about what is painless and beautiful, undemanding and open-ended, an adjunct of the modern assumption that happiness is the purpose of life on earth. So to Christianity recast as ethicism is added Christianity as personal therapy. How far this all is from the message of the Saviour! God was in the world when Jesus walked the hills of Galilee and when he wept over the city of Jerusalem; his message to humanity can be known with certainty because he came among us to teach and to live the spiritual life. And that message begins with the dreadful fact of human sin and the need for individual repentance. Nothing in the intervening two millennia has altered that. The Christian religion is centred in the worship of God and the surrender of human wills to the divine purposes. It was never intended to become the sugared palliative of humanity's sense of its own worth.

One Hundred and Sixteen

———

Christmas cheer

ಐ೦ಚ

Christmas is a time for giving. God's gift of his Son is echoed in our giving tokens of our affection or regard to those whom we love or know. But it is a transaction: we also receive. And that makes the simple exchange a more complicated matter than at first appears. For to be a good receiver requires self-conscious understanding. In today's society people – most people, at any rate in Western society – possess so much, and expect so much, that receiving has become routinized. We have lost a sense of gratitude for much that we receive, taking for granted benefits and possessions which in former conditions of society, and in many parts of the developing world now, would be regarded with awe. Jesus commended the poor who give all that they have. Like the lost sheep and the lost coin in the parables he was reminding us that the value in giving and in receiving is not defined by worldly estimates but by cost in relation to the people involved. The virtue of giving requires the reciprocation of receiving. Consider how this otherwise rather trite observation actually works in reality. Most gifts we make to others are not actual objects, like a toy to a child; they are gifts of time and emotional engagement. We bother with another person in some moment when they are experiencing stress or disappointment in circumstances that are often undramatic, often seemingly trivial. But it is a gift nonetheless, and one which many of us do not bother to make when we have the opportunity to do so. Receiving such commonplace gifts needs awareness on our part, too. We should not take the attentions or kindnesses of others for granted.

231

Christmas is about the gift of God's love: God so loved the world that he *gave* his only begotten son. That, too, requires our response. We must know how to receive that love. The teaching of Jesus himself is clear; we can show that we have received God's love by loving one another. But what does that mean in daily life? The fact is that humans are fallen creatures, often with extremely vile characteristics. The supremacy of God's love enfolds men and women, but how can *we* rise to such sublime heights? Loving your neighbours is all very well when they seem agreeable; what happens, however, when they are (as humans all are) feckless, mean-minded, faithless? That is precisely where the Christian religion is seen to be an affair not of sentiment and emotional indulgence but becomes what it truly is – a painful discipline which goes against the grain of our self-seeking. Everyone can love a saint, but it takes a saint to love a sinner. In Christ's religion, however, everyone can become a saint, and that, also, is celebrated at Christmas time. For the first witnesses of God's gift were all kinds of people: simple shepherds in the fields, who left their flocks to find the child in the manger; and wise men who gave up their expectations of majesty to acknowledge the King whose birth was shadowed by a crown of thorns. Giving and receiving: God's gift conveyed in our hands.

_____

Millennium blues

Enough of the millennium. The various celebrations have amusingly served only to confirm how trivial and debased are this generation's beliefs about the purpose of life on earth: a mishmash of cultural relativism, of representations of mere human accomplishments as 'spiritual' values, of self-interested materialism dressed up as compassion. So let us turn instead to the next thousand years.

Modern people are obsessed by the pursuit of personal security, and this is extended into fears about the future of the planet itself. In the past there was a general acceptance that human life was frail, that the world was a hazardous place, and that risk was inseparable from advance. Indeed, it is arguable that much nobility derived from scorning danger. Today we are suffocatingly enveloped in a culture of health and safety; ecological preoccupations stimulate a materialist world-picture which is, paradoxically, thought of as quintessentially 'moral'. Now the Bible presents us with a hugely different view of things. There the world is described as being in a process of transition – from creation to destruction – and human life is depicted as inseparably linked with the fate of all things. Men and women are granted the faculties of reason and reflection, but their status as creatures remains unaltered, and in the biblical account there is an acceptance that they are subject to the dynamics of growth and the certainty of decay, like everything else. A large part of the teaching of Jesus concerned judgement: time, too, is thus rendered in finite images – the earth is moving towards a cataclysmic end, just as each individual life terminates in the personal cataclysm of death. We now know, due to successful scientific investigation, that human life and its terrestrial vehicle exist in the middle of a monstrous explosion: the universe, also, is a momentary phenomenon, and our sense of time is as a frame caught in extreme slow-motion. Perhaps the next thousand years will see the end of our planet, or of the human life which coats its surface so tenuously. And perhaps it will not. There is no way of knowing. What can be calculated are some of the possibilities. Will the earth come to an end through collision with another piece of space debris? Will there be nuclear warfare following proliferation of weapons and technology? Will humanity succumb to commonplace diseases because drugs become increasingly ineffective? Will terrifying new viruses evolve, which may kill us all off? Will there be a massive breakdown of order in society produced by conditions of crisis as yet unimagined? It is not very comforting. But then the Saviour did not promise worldly comfort; he spoke, instead, of appalling events to come, when the skies would be darkened and the dead would rise up from their graves. 'Watch and pray' – these were the words for the future which Christ himself taught us. How many will mark the start of the new millennium by doing just that? Humanity is set upon an adventurous and dangerous course of discovery, called by God himself to share in the progressive development of the earth, and perhaps, also, to reach out to places beyond. The world's sorrows are nothing to that. 'Be of good cheer,' Jesus said, 'I have overcome the world.'

One Hundred and Eighteen

Human disobedience

ೞೞೞ

There has been an explosion of knowledge in our times, an enormous expansion of information about the nature of life and the context in which it is set. But the quality of the wisdom available to men and women has not changed. And nor, it must be emphasized, has the timeless level of human sin – the chasm between what we can conceive as goodness and the ability we possess to deliver it. Unfortunately people today seem disposed to expect perfection, and when they discover that this is not in correspondence with reality they pit themselves angrily against those whom they identify as the agents of their frustration. This is evidenced, for example, in attitudes to military conflict. The television images of ordinary human nastiness that is (and always has been) inseparable from warfare are unacceptable to the sanitized consciences of modern people – who demand the results of force without actually using the means of coercion. Or it is seen in the resort to law to criminalize petty human failings of the sort which human nature will forever furnish: the result is the demonizing of the weak and the sensationalizing of tragic defects in men and women who just cannot cope. To be wise is to discriminate with available knowledge, and to recognize that the capacity to act is not permission to act. Human wisdom is like spiritual formation – it has to be cultivated through life. It requires points of reference in individual character which are not variable or relative; it is, indeed, a gift of God.

Humans are called, by their very nature, to share in the divine scheme for the development of the life of the planet –

235

and perhaps (who knows?) eventually to reach out to the extraordinary creation beyond. They have, that is to say, the capacities of reason and reflection which afford them a measure of moral inventiveness. But the God who created them also made himself known to them, partly through their reasoned exploration of the nature of reality and partly in religious revelation. Both these means indicate that men and women are not sovereign over themselves. Reality shows this when natural catastrophe convulses our expectation of safety and stability; religion tells us this in the laws which God intimates through the traditions of believers. We are not free agents. God calls us to share in the progressive development of the earth on his terms – and not according to our demands, corrupted as they are by the intrinsic frailties of human nature. There is a limit to how far humans may go; there is a line beyond which God's will for creation cannot be crossed. It is becoming truly difficult in our day to discern exactly where that line is. Yet it *is* there. How far can we use the expanding pool of knowledge to engineer life itself? To what extent should human inventiveness set terms to the procreation of life, to its preservation, to its termination? To what extent are we applying knowledge simply to match our goals of painlessness and comfort at the expense of moral conduct? Christians believe that humans are *not* sovereign over their own bodies, and nor are they morally autonomous. Knowledge without wisdom is the seat of human pride, and it always has been. Our problem today is our sheer ability to magnify our rebellion against spiritual constraints. Jesus called us to repentance. If we do not listen to him we shall multiply our errors and make a living hell of reality.

One Hundred and Nineteen

The kingdom of heaven is at hand

ℰ☙ℭ

It is the beginning of Holy Week, when Christians, even more than at other times, remember that it is *their* sins which caused the sufferings and death of Jesus. Here is the central mystery in the Christian understanding of God: not the miracle of the Incarnation, not the splendour of Christ's earthly ministry, not even the majesty of the Resurrection – but that the Creator of all things should bother with people like us. Human sin is not an accidental by-product of the way we live, or the conse-quence of wrong social conditioning. Nor is it the disregard of moral obligations which men and women have over time delivered in response to their desires. Sin is inseparable from our natures, and it issues from faults in ourselves which we cannot put right through our own efforts. Christianity recog-nizes this. It is not a religion for those who seek to reconstruct a perfect version of humanity, purged of evil and in control of its own destiny. It regards such utopianism – widely implicit in modern attitudes to the capacity of humans to order their own affairs – as simply unrealistic. Christianity is about forgiveness. God forgives human sin. If we reach out to him he will forgive each one of us: the formally virtuous, the depraved, the morally unlovely, the despairing. There is no tariff for our sins; the gift of forgiveness is free. Since no one deserves forgiveness, and no one has even the beginnings of the means of self-correction, the sacrifice of Christ is wholly a gift, the most perfect gift the world will ever know. Holy Week is a good time to devote a

------

237

moment of reflection on each of its days to recollect our own catalogue of personal sin. When he was in the world Jesus spoke most about the need for men and women to repent. But modern people do not feel the need for repentance. For this is an age of self-esteem, when people dwell upon their rights and exalt their moral freedom; when even religion is embraced as a means of achieving individual emotional benefits, as a kind of therapy, rather than as an act of surrender to the sovereign demands of God. It is hard for those to repent who do not believe they are corrupted. Holy Week, therefore, is also a time of sorrow. The sins of the world lie grimly around us, their evidence never further away than our own actions and neglects. The priceless gift of life, taken for granted, becomes a desert of wastes, as the lost opportunities stack up, and the light handed to us by Christ grows dim in our keeping. What greater sorrow can there be than to realize that it was *our* sins which produced the death of Christ? Yet what more serene happiness is there than the receipt of the forgiveness which the same Christ holds out to those who repent?

The whole concept of repentance needs fresh representation in this generation. The disasters which interrupt the human love of security and material welfare, and which formerly reduced men and women to contrition, no longer do so. Today, in contrast, it is not the awesome presence of God which people see in catastrophe: indeed, virtually any kind of affliction is now taken as evidence there can be no God at all. People cannot imagine a being who could possibly 'allow' human suffering. What vanity! We are now a people who make their own sense of the divine dependent upon the maintenance of their material well-being. Holy Week is truly a time for reflection on the horror of our own natures.

One Hundred and Twenty

Triumph over death

ℰℭ

The Resurrection of Christ was a real and corporeal event. It seems strange to have to emphasize this, but it has to be recorded that many Christians now interpret the Resurrection as a matter of symbolism and imagery. The followers of Jesus, they suppose, experienced the presence of his love after his physical death – he had, so to speak, returned to them in the experience of their fellowship. The teaching authority of the Church, however, has always rejected this contention, which has been put forward in some manner or other from the very beginning. It is no part of Christianity. Jesus rose from the dead, and it was the real and actual Christ whom the disciples proclaimed to the world: theirs was the cult of one who had triumphed over death, and it was this conviction, not some metaphor, which spread throughout the peoples. We read in Scripture itself that 'some doubted', and the biblical narratives recount that the followers of Jesus himself sometimes did not recognize his resuscitated appearance. But these are not possible evidences that could be used to undermine the veracity of the Church's teaching, for the Gospels were not written to provide accounts of the life of Jesus, but to *prove* that he was the Christ. They are not a series of objective compilations of the sort we may expect to sustain a modern television documentary but the testimony of those who already believed. The Gospels, in consequence, cannot furnish *any* internal evidence to indicate that the believers of the early Church were mistaken in their faith. The Resurrection of Christ is the foundation of the Christian religion.

Christianity is not established by the immediate personal experience of individual believers, it is not based in the emotions. It is the acceptance as truth of the testimony of those who through successive centuries, and in different cultures, have received the assurance of the first disciples. We depend on the reliability of this tradition of the believers for all our knowledge of salvation – not only the literal fact of the Resurrection but *all* the teachings about God imparted to men by the mercy of Christ. It is not for us to pick and choose, according to sensibilities or tastes conditioned by the needs and priorities and intellectual dispositions of each age. It is certainly our duty to represent those truths in the available language and symbolism of each age, but not to eliminate dimensions of the faith which seem incompatible with transient modes of cultural understanding. One of the failings of the present time, in fact, is to render religious belief as a species of emotional satisfaction: a given teaching or practice is accepted or rejected on the basis that it tends or does not tend to enhance emotional need, aesthetic sense, or the intellectual fastidiousness of individuals. Yet Jesus was not concerned with such requisites. His searing references, on the contrary, were to human corruption, the need for repentance, the certainty of judgement. It is not possible to believe in him as Saviour of the world without accepting the *whole* testimony of those who first proclaimed his truth. He was not, to them, a mere ethical teacher but the one who conquered death. Rejoice, this Easter, that belief in Christ does not rest on human understanding but on our submission to the divine will.

Universal sin

ജ

During the last few decades Christian leaders have particularly associated their faith with the pursuit of justice – usually defined in terms of social policy, world distribution of resources, and human rights. This new century has opened with a vigorous determination to 'see justice done' over past violations of human rights in a number of prominent cases. Thus Jewish agencies have hunted down former Nazis, and the arrest of General Pinochet of Chile in London was used by pressure groups to establish new principles of law in relation to human rights crimes. But there are moral problems in these proceedings which should cause some unease. The prosecution of recent violations of human rights is plainly more satisfactory than the pursuit of offences which occurred many years ago: memories are untainted by recent developments of opinion, witnesses are more reliable, and, above all, the moral culture in which the hearings take place is the same. The prosecutors of those guilty of offences in the various Balkan operations, for example, have a clarity impossible for offences committed many years ago. Whereas it is true that there are moral absolutes – murder is always murder – it is not the case that the circumstances are of equal value in determining the degree of culpability, the extent of ideological motivation (as against ordinary personal wickedness), or the extent to which the actions of the victorious side in a past conflict become evaluated as 'acceptable force', while those of the defeated become 'war crimes'. Surely there must be insuperable difficulties when an alleged criminal whose actions took place fifty years ago is brought to account now? It can never be justice to try a man according to the beliefs and passions of a later age. Sex crimes of the past, prosecuted in today's climate of moral hysteria, raise the same difficulties.

Somewhere there needs to be a line, a moment of forgiveness. This is especially needed where the prosecutors of a distant crime are themselves descendants of the defeated side in an earlier conflict. For them, the pursuit of justice easily passes into revenge. Christianity has much to say about the priority of forgiveness over the evil of revenge. Revenge may be as sinful as the original crime. 'How often shall my brother sin against me, and I forgive him?' Jesus was asked, by those who based forgiveness on a legal calculation. Jesus, in his mercy, replied that forgiveness was without limitation. This must especially apply when the offences concerned are full of evidential uncertainty, decades old, and are being investigated on one side only by hostile and well-financed agencies. At a certain point we always let go of the past; if we did not, social life would become an intolerable jungle of remembered grievances. The notion that there is an educative value in perpetrating the memory of distant inhumanities, as a sort of deterrent to future occurrences, is simply unrealistic. Modern people cannot cope with the fact – for fact it is – that humans behave nastily. They will always do so. Their horrifying conduct is not the consequence of false ideology but of their unregenerate natures. Wickedness will work through any ideology: first we need to seek to address the natures of men and women, and then the ideologies they assemble and enact will have more beneficial effects. Forgiveness derives from the supervening mercy of God. Let the dead bury their dead, and let us live in the land of the living.

Living with sin

ഔരു

Christians believe that they are owned by God, and that they are responsible to him for the use of their earthly bodies. Made in his image, their nature is to receive a relationship with God; being 'like' God means being able to communicate with him. This communication does not resemble a human conversation: it is established by doing his will. When we cease to communicate we are liable to be in a condition of sin. This is all elementary Christianity – once (but no longer) taught to children in school. We are stewards of our bodies and not the owners. It is therefore a Christian duty to strive for mastery of the body, to learn how to subdue its passions, to control emotions, and to recognize that what the tradition of past Christian believers has passed to us about God's will for how we live is still valid. How fearfully old-fashioned this all sounds in an age of shameless self-indulgence! We parade a range of euphemisms and self-deceptions to justify our moral illiteracy: indulgence is not indulgence but a 'healthy' attitude to affirming life. Some women who regard pregnancy as an interference with their lifestyle choose abortion as 'a woman's *right*'. More commonly, people have come to dissociate sexual congress from moral considerations at all: it has come to be accepted as what people in 'a relationship' do to express pleasure. Many bishops of the Church of England now appear to favour the remarriage of the divorced by the Church even though the Church's own teaching prohibits divorce. Why? Because the priority of human love is perceived to overrule moral law – a latter-day exemplification of what used in the

1960s to be called 'situational ethics'. Mastery over the body finds few advocates today. It is thought a violation of individual choice to advise people of moral laws which are intended precisely for situations where the passions overwhelm piety.

Now there are some areas of human nature in which the advance of knowledge may legitimately lead to changed attitudes. Perhaps the Church's teaching on homosexuality, for example, is in such a category. This is different in kind from the marriage discipline, where the Church upholds a sacramental bond freely entered into, and points to the violation of an oath if there is a dissolution. Homosexuality appears to be a gift from God, an involuntary condition; it is how some are made, and for them moral conduct has to be observed within an alternative set of references. Mastery over the body applies to persons of all types of sexuality, however. Now is it possible to distinguish morally between different expressions of sexuality? This is a difficult and controversial area, and where there have always been relative judgements mixed up with the absolutes. The age of consent for sexual relations, for example, has varied throughout time – the modern, fairly late age would be considered extraordinary by most of our predecessors. The modern Church of England has a horror of controversy, and tends to allow the agenda for the debate about sexual morality to be set by the humanist moral sense of media opinion. It is only too easy to allow the base gratification of human need to be accepted as a kind of healthy recognition of human love. Those who dare to counsel the wisdom of traditional moral knowledge are not highly regarded in the modern culture of consumer sex. And some who call for free choice about unwanted pregnancies, for example, do not seem to be concerned about moral law, but about disposing of a social problem.

One Hundred and Twenty Three

————

Ruler of the heart

&⁂ઝ

Two of the most common misunderstandings of the Christian faith are sadly to be found as much among those inside as among those outside the Church. They are the reduction of religion to a mere set of ethical principles, and the supposition that religious belief is founded upon personal emotional need. Both attitudes humanize the Faith, converting it into an extension of the desire which men and women have to achieve a life on earth which is safe and satisfying. Yet at the heart of the message of Jesus is the dreadful fact of human sin. The world of his day was filled with wonderful ethical systems – some of them, indeed, like the Greek pursuit of a balanced social order, achieving the highest thought. But individual lives were still imprisoned in sin. The ethics taught by Jesus comprised measures which gave content to the spiritual life, and they were entirely dependent upon it. The ethics of Jesus were not, therefore, the centre of his teaching – which was to do with an intrinsic disorder in human life. His great gift to humanity was not an ethical system but personal forgiveness to those who repent. Christianity is a religion of obedience to the divine will, and it is designed for a race who are incapable, through ethical systems or legal devices, to regenerate themselves. Those who are forgiven have then the obligation to try to practise the spiritual life by adopting the ethical principles which Jesus taught to illustrate the nature of the kingdom. No one can earn redemption by *behaviour*, however exalted and well-intentioned. It is not behaviour but *belief* which presages redemption. The gateway to eternal life is

————

245

discerned by those who recognize their sinfulness and believe in the sovereignty of God. The gate is narrow and the way is hard. But Christianity is a religion for sinners; those for whom the vision of paradise is opened are often those whom the world scorns because of their poor behaviour. Yet God upholds them, in all their ethical frailty, because of their belief.

The way to redemption is not established in human emotional need either. Just as ethical behaviour tests the faith of believers and gives it content in the world, so aesthetic sensation and emotional satisfaction may accompany faith but are not themselves of the substance of faith. We offer the best we can contrive to God when we worship him – in music, words, art and design. But our faith will be empty if it is founded upon these merely human accomplishments. They are also highly relative to time and circumstance. People who give up going to church because 'it did nothing for me' were probably there for the wrong reasons in the first place. Presence in church is an expression of being incorporated into the body of the Lord in the world – it has nothing to do with emotional or aesthetic satisfaction. Religion is not therapy. It is about the rule of God in individual lives. It is extremely hard for modern people to accept the fact of personal sinfulness, and the religion of Christ, which is based on the prior confession of sin, has little appeal in consequence. It is scarcely necessary to look any further to account for the decline in the numbers of those attending church. It would be helpful if Christians themselves sorted out their priorities, and started to realize that the Christ whom they declare to the world is not an emotional impulse but a living Lord.

One Hundred and Twenty Four

———

More than a token

෪෬

The Christian life is centred in the Holy Eucharist, the service of blessing and thanksgiving offered to God in perpetuation of the great supper of the Lord before his sacrifice for our sins. It is also called the mass, or 'missa', to indicate that the followers of Christ are being sent out to teach his truth. The Eucharist is thus the authority of the mission of the people of God, a personal and collective participation in the death of Jesus and the mystery of redemption. It is only secondarily, and by contingence, an affair of human fellowship, where believers share bread and wine as a kind of love-feast memorial of Christ – though that is the aspect of the Eucharist which many Christians today emphasize. The truth and authenticity of Christianity, however, do not depend upon the *experience* of faith among believers (which is the essence of Protestantism in its Evangelical representation) but on the succession of teaching derived from those who stand in the tradition of the apostles. And the apostles had themselves first received the body of the Lord and handed on the knowledge of his objective presence in the Eucharist. Christians believe that when the priest celebrates the holy rite Christ himself exists among them, as he descends to the earth veiled from human sight in the forms of bread and wine. This is the most solemn moment in Christian worship, the very union of heaven and earth, always to be venerated, never to be received except in awe and unutterable gratitude.

The Holy Eucharist is also the sublime symbol of the communion of the faithful with the greater company of heaven.

By submitting to Christ in the world Christians already become citizens of the unseen kingdom of the blessed – who beckon them to eternity, and safeguard their way. No one who joins the Church of Christ is ever alone. If the world no longer seems to provide companionship or human love – as so many feel – the citizenship of eternity, encountered at the Eucharist, does. To join in the *missa* of Christ is to be integrated with the mysterious presence of a vast society. This may all sound a bit 'churchy', and so it is. Christ did not deliver his truth to a form of words or a written text. Even the sacred books of Scripture bear their authority because selected by the early Church to be received as the Word of God. Christ did not found a school of thought or a philosophical system, as so many teachers of the ancient world did. He entrusted his truth to a people: to us. We are its guardians and interpreters; what human society will know of him is what existing believers convey in their teaching. And there is the core significance of the Holy Eucharist and of the mission of the Church; the Eucharist purchased our redemption and authorizes our truth. We, shamefully, are forever inclined to reduce this priceless gift to mere personal consolation, a means of self-understanding, individual therapy, a celebration of human camaraderie, a beautiful experience. But the message of Jesus is blood and nails, ripping flesh and the execration of the multitude. The Eucharist is not a piece of sentimental drama; it is the actual presence of Christ amongst those he came to save. Happy are those who are called to such a feast.

One Hundred and Twenty Five

_____

Moral confusion

ᏚᎧᏟᏃ

If puritanism may be defined as the regulation by authority of the details of private life then we are indeed living in an age of puritanism. Puritanism is especially evidenced when interventions are justified on moral grounds. Christians today should be worried because the morality being enforced is a rival to their own – though they are usually unaware of this because it bears a resemblance to Christian ethical principle, and is a sort of simulation and replacement of it. Christian leaders, in fact, often identify their faith with many secular provisions which represent themselves as being – and may actually be – concerned with human welfare. But welfare and Christian morality do not always coincide. A woman may, with considerable public support, regard it as for her welfare that she procures an abortion, but that can hardly be judged welfare for the unborn life which is discarded. Or a person may be 'taken into care' (or seized by the state, to put it more bluntly) when the family deem it an inconvenience to have them around. There are difficult and painful issues of judgement here. But it is certainly unwise to assume that perceived welfare and Christian morality can always be identified as operating in sympathy.

The moral compulsion of the new puritanism is operating within the undefined relativism of 'the plural society': its moral pedigree is left unstated. No one cares to define the moral philosophy of which it is the detailed blueprint. There is simply an assumption that all enlightened people will agree, as if the authority of the new moral puritanism was self-evident – a kind of Natural Law. It is, indeed, possible to put forward such a justification; but this is rarely attempted, and the moral crudity revealed by politicians who try it is not a pretty sight. Like the august structure of 'political correctness', which is the secular catechism of the new puritanism, it is usually described in terms of welfare provision. It is the substitute for religious belief, not its embodiment. To take Christian moral formulations as the basis for public morality, as in the past, is regarded as sectarian, and an affront to those in the nation whose beliefs are not Christian. It is doubtful if in reality the new puritanism has a basis in ethnicity, nor is it democratic. It is the work of a humanist élite, many of whom are unaware of the real philosophical pedigree of their ideas.

The result, however, is a progressive diminution of the area of individual liberty – whether in the capacity of parents to care for their children without excessive interventions by agencies of the state, or in the ideas about race or gender which individuals may express. The intentions are laudable; the result is a tyranny of opinion. Christians should worry because the space needed for the free adoption of religious ideas and practices is being taken over by the state – usually under the euphemism of 'regulation'. Some of this is probably beneficial and necessary; a lot of it robs the individual of the ability to exercise free moral choice. The creation of totalitarianism is always disturbing, but it is especially disquieting when it occurs without the declaration of an identifiable ideology – which can be attacked by its opponents – and when its moral absolutism is presented as self-evident welfare. Step by step we are passing into the realm of unfreedom, and sadly the Churches are benignly acquiescent. The notion, also, that human wrongdoing can be eliminated by regulatory legislation is simply unrealistic. People are intrinsically flawed. They need the forgiveness of God rather than the strictures of men.

———

Raised to glory

ഇൗൽ

The Ascension of Christ, celebrated by Christians on Thursday, was a demonstration of the splendour and supreme authority of God. The risen Christ was then revealed in majesty, time and eternity were joined, the seen and the unseen worlds opened to the gaze of men. Here was Jesus in the light of the heavenly presence, who had illuminated the world and now was drawn to a perfection beyond the world's understanding. The images that can be appreciated by mortals were exceeded by the actual event, as Jesus passed from his humanity to his divinity – always one, and always of transcendent spiritual beauty, as he holds out to the least lovely of his creatures the priceless gift of eternal citizenship. The modern world notably lacks images of splendour, having come to settle for merely human priorities. It is now difficult, within our cultural references, to imagine the intimations of the divine presence; there are no longer splendid courts or exalted rulers whose style simulates on earth projections of supreme authority. Our human accomplishments, often these days falsely described as 'spiritual values' – like art and music – are a mean substitute for the presence of God. Our daily lives, bereft of religious references of the sort which in traditional societies marked the passage of time, are preoccupied with apparent urgencies which, like the thorns in the Parable of the Sower, exclude authentic spiritual formation.

So let us look again at the fact of the Ascension: Christ in majesty. Christians love and obey Jesus not for what he did for them, not even in the gift of redemption. They certainly do not love him because of any 'meaning' he may give to their lives, or any 'uplift' they may suppose they experience. They love him for himself. Jesus is the eternal God; to be known and feared because of his authority as Creator, to be respected as the author of moral law, to be obeyed because humans are his property. But also, and above all, Jesus is to be loved. Earthly love is a shadow of the divine love, and may educate men and women in some of its preliminaries. Earthly love, however, is deceptive and unreliable: it offers paradise yet delivers an ambiguous mixture of exultation and disappointment. Even when it seems stable it has in reality become merely routinized. We like to think that our love of others, or of another, is unconditional – but that is never really so. Our love of God, if it is truly in us, really is without limitation or reservation, as is God's love for us. So greatly did he love the work of his hands – which he had placed in an environment of such hazard and potential sorrow, but where we receive a nurturing in eternal citizenship – that he died for our salvation. If we would see the power of that love we should behold the Christ of the Ascension: the final demonstration of the divine truth that goodness overcomes evil, and that the partial values of the world have their perfection in the kingdom that is everlasting. Rejoice at being called to know such a Saviour; be amazed that the frailty of our love is met by the supreme love of God.

Wrong perspectives

ഔ౧౪

A young child dies in a house fire; thousands perish in an earthquake; a virus deprives a young man of his future; a baby is born dead. The question so frequently asked by this generation is 'Can there be a God when such things happen?' The sense that commonplace events like these are an outrage against human entitlements prompts many to scepticism or complete atheism; indeed the apparent arbitrariness of life is probably the chief cause of defection from religious belief today. People suppose their moral instincts about the fate of others – not to speak of themselves – are higher than those of a Divinity who can afflict such horrors upon a race they have been told he loves. The just and the unjust, furthermore, are equally subject to the chances of life. The good and the bad are liable to suffer in balanced numbers. But to question the existence of a benign God as the basis of such evidence – which was equally available to the countless millions of religious believers who have preceded us on the planet – is simply a piece of human vanity. We have too high an estimate of our own value. The moral sense of the modern world is centred in our claims to an existence which is free of suffering; we regard it as unacceptable if our material welfare is not judged the supreme consideration. Thus people today are anchored by authentic materialism: they see themselves as most truly 'spiritual' when they regard the material 'care' of others as more important than the values and beliefs which all of us exist to discover. They love humanity above the love of God. And presumably they also imagine that men and women are so

253

possessed of inherent goodness that they really are entitled to a pain-free existence.

Yet God has willed things differently. The scriptural accounts of the creation, though symbolical, do lay out great truths. One of these, in a way the most obvious, is that God created the world for his own (and unknowable) purposes, and saw that it was good for those purposes. The world, as part of an exploding universe, is transient and unstable, and the creatures which generated upon its surface are subject to the same processes of chance and change as everything else. Dust you are, God told humanity, and to dust you shall return. The works of God's hands, being creatures and not the Creator, are lesser beings and they are intrinsically flawed. Jesus came into the world not because humanity is good and lovely, and can expect nothing but happiness in life, but because men and women are corrupted in their natures and are unable in their own strengths to achieve amendment. Their lives are *not* their own, but are leased to them for a short term and on explicit conditions. Education in spirituality comes through experience of the world, the good and the evil which happen to men and women comprising the divine curriculum. The earth is a place of trial, not a safe resting place. It is our vanity which produces our yearning for a reality stripped of its content, our sense of self-worth which demands that we shall have whatever we ask. But God is the sovereign of all things, and we are called to trust him. To doubt his providence is a great sin.

One Hundred and Twenty Eight

The mirror of
imperfection

ಬಿಂಕಿ

People are very tiresome. This may be disagreeable to have to confess: but if we ignore reality we shall deceive ourselves. Anyone who is cheerily optimistic about humanity is simply liable to false judgement. People are not very nice. Yet made by God to have a companionship with him, and called by God to be the stewards of the earth, men and women are capable of a kind of greatness; they are disordered versions of perfection. They can imagine moral splendour but cannot deliver it, even in the most trivial aspects of daily life. They are created as spiritual beings, yet their exercise of their spiritual faculties actually becomes a compound of vanity: in place of intimations of celestial values they interpose the individual pursuit of personal significance and the aesthetic sensations derived from human accomplishments. Their concern for the welfare of others, elevated enough in relation to those with whom they are linked by immediate ties of affection, is flawed by self-interest and a curious censoriousness about those whose taste for good works is not commensurate with their own. Human life has dignity, for it is a gift of God. But we as individuals do not. The expressions 'human dignity' and 'the sanctity of human life', when properly used, describe qualities imparted to us by God – qualities we frequently misuse or choose to ignore; they do not describe what we are actually like. God's gift of the dignity of life is entrusted to us for the span of a lifetime: the extent to which we employ it to make ourselves dignified is up to each

255

one of us. The record of accomplishment is not good. Jesus always spoke of humanity as in need of radical change – nothing less than the complete rejection of our corrupted wills, and the attendant wrong priorities, and our submission to the sovereignty of God. Time and time again, however, each one of us makes our own desires the sovereign of our lives. Then our potential for dignity slips away, and our tiresomeness passes into sin.

Yet Jesus did not come into the world to condemn the world, but to offer men and women the prospect of salvation. And there is the authentic dignity of humanity. It is the *gift* of life which is sacred; our lives may be touched by its sanctity through our pursuit of the divine purpose. Instead, we interpret life as a matter of rights and entitlements, with ourselves as the beneficiaries, not of an eternal citizenship, but of immediate worldly rewards: the treasure is stored up on earth. Even so, the eternal splendour flickers dimly in the life of everyone, for Jesus called each one to be his follower. That light will illuminate the whole of ourselves if we submit to God's will. Men and women are not transformed thereby: their corrupted humanity remains – but they are *forgiven*. Self-seeking and greedy, an unhappy affliction to others and an *habitué* of sin: people are nevertheless the raw materials of the kingdom of Christ. First, we must rid ourselves of false sentimentality about humanity. We are not very satisfactory; we are given to wickedness; we embrace wrong priorities. Modern society, when all the humanist euphemisms are discarded, is shabbily unacquainted with the pursuit of higher purposes – a projection of the inherent human craving to settle for material rather than spiritual goals. Yet look into the face of another and you will see the face of Christ: a face of sorrow, awaiting the act of contrition which restores dignity. This is the indwelling Christ, who awaits recognition by us – so great is his patience and his love.

Clear advice

 BOCB

It is quite rare these days to hear a sermon about sexual morality. This is extraordinary since we live at a time when sex is exhibited in so many public ways – in television dramas and discussions, in advertising, in school programmes of 'moral' teaching. The agenda for debate of human sexuality is set by the media, and it is thoroughly secularized; the clergy appear to *follow* its main lines in such advice as they do offer. It is the secular moralists, medical experts, and the hosts of care workers who define the various issues. The Church of the past was not silent on these matters, nor is the Catholic Church today – despite the apparent rejection of its teaching by so many of its lay adherents, claiming a right to 'think for themselves'. The pulpits of the Victorian era we imagine to have been thunderously precise in declamations about sexual morality, though later caricatures, serving later inclinations to simplify the past, cloud judgement of the matter. How is it possible to account for the reticence of the Church of England of today? Why do the preachers opt for discourses about Third World poverty rather than the rules of sexuality? Sex, after all, involves the most familiar forms in which individuals encounter moral choice. The answer probably lies in a horror of controversy. Church leaders abhor any rocking of the boat. Yet virtually everything which is intellectually serious provokes dispute, so everything is controversial. There is also a paradox: progressive choice in sexual morality falls within an acceptable liberal consensus, whereas 'traditional' teaching is perceived to be controversial unless it can be firmly identified as 'family values'. The teaching of Jesus was divisive; he did not set out to establish a consensus and spoke of his truth as bringing a sword – and that brother would be divided against brother. There is no intellectual advance without the testing of propositions, and in the process the boat is rocked all the time. If the Church would fulfil its prophetic calling it should give up avoiding controversy. The leaders are delighted with themselves when they risk incurring unpopularity, as they suppose, by supporting the claims to social justice of various groups: so why can't they say something clear, if unpopular, about abortion?

Now human sexuality is a controversial area precisely because there have been great advances of knowledge. Some practices once considered vile are now, because shown to be built into people by conditions over which they have no control, correctly considered acceptable. Some sexual impulsions, long judged vile, are always vile: adultery, for example, or sex with animals. In some matters technology has intervened, and a whole secondary realm of moral ambiguity has opened up. Difficult decisions are needed: but often the leaders of the Protestant Churches simply decline to give a lead, even to their own followers. How many people know that the Church of England, in its formal teaching, condemns both divorce and abortion? They rarely hear those matters taught in the pulpit except as open 'issues' about which there is current public debate – thus, once again, implicitly accepting the validity of the secular moral agenda. Church leaders have a duty to advise their own church members about the law of the Church, and to make sure that they have got it clear themselves. They also have a duty to assist in extending modern knowledge about human sexuality. The two are not incompatible.

One Hundred and Thirty

———

Sacrifice

ଛଠଓଷ

Pride is a great inventor of religion. We set up ourselves and our needs and then select religious beliefs which cater for them; our souls are fed a diet of self-satisfaction. We seek a God who will flatter our self-esteem; who will grant our wish to find meaning and purpose in life; who will preside over a personal universe of ordered and uninterrupted happiness; whose ways are our ways; whose provisions meet our wants; whose laws we can easily obey without personal cost. The religion of modern people demonstrates their exercise of individualized sovereignty: it is the aspiration of those who recognize no discipline beyond their own judgement. This is a religion fashioned by emotional indulgence, selected from available beliefs by chance decision. It is the projection of a craving for generalized and sentimentalized regard for humanity – not as it is, corrupted and morally frail, but as people yearn for it to be: an idealized extension of their own sense of self-worth. Today's religion hopes to achieve a sense of beauty and spiritual repose; a therapy exercise derived from an interior world hugely at variance with the actual world experienced by our predecessors in traditional society – who were not insulated from reality by the comforts of modern lifestyles and sanitized death. Human life envisaged by today's religious entrepreneurs is all Goodness and Truth and Human Virtue: a check-list of generalities without observable content, detached from the nastiness of living and breathing people, and unrelated to the possibilities for evil lurking in daily social exchange. It is astonishing that after millennia of human development the men and women of

259

today, with all their knowledge of the material workings of the planet, and their intellectual resources, should reveal themselves to be so juvenile in their understanding of what authentic religion is all about. They really do seem to think it is a phenomenon of the emotions, a matter of beautiful experience – rather like bourgeois appreciation of art.

Consider, in terrible contrast, the torn flesh and the excruciating reality of the man on the Cross. Now there is true religion: the death of the man of innocence at the hands of the sinful, a cosmic drama representing an eternal act of mercy – as the Creator of all things purchased redemption for a people who were certainly, by any worldly assessment, not worth it. True religion is about sacrifice and personal pain, discipline and offering, the disgusting yet spiritually cleansing service of the unclean and rejected. It is about the things we do *not* want to do, and it derives from beliefs that are not pleasant to have to believe. At the foot of the Cross we are very far from the therapy religion of modern society; there we are confronted not with conventional beauty and serene experience, but with the Saviour of the world in agony. This is not the easy vision of the moralists and their human panaceas: it is the world we are called by Christ to serve face to face. The greatest service we can offer to others is not the short-term palliation of material applications but the knowledge of salvation. This is religion with real demands, for it goes against our self-regarding instincts and causes us pain. The gate is narrow and the way is hard; those who try to discern the way need the help of Christ himself, and it is his suffering which, in the act of acceptance, is converted into joy.